NOT SO PRETTY IN PINK

Christi Odom Maynard

Copyright © 2015 Ms. Christi Odom Maynard
All rights reserved.

ISBN: 151436395X
ISBN 13: 9781514363959

CHAPTER ONE

It is something that we all think about. If you say that it has never crossed your mind, you would be lying. You are at a party or an event, and you see someone without his or her hair. It is a very uncomfortable feeling. Looking at this person, you say to yourself, I wonder what kind of cancer. A very scary feeling comes over you, and you can't help but put yourself there. Could that be me? Cancer has touched all of us in some way or another. Honestly, these days it's all too close for comfort for anyone. If we all stop our daily activities and truly think about what is going on around us, cancer is rapidly taking over. We can all keep our heads in the sand, but the truth of the matter is that cancer is bigger than me or you.

I never knew how much until now. The day my life changed was the day I promised God that if he would allow me to live, I would do everything in my power to make a difference in the world. You know, we all should know we have a purpose in this beautiful world we live in. The part that is hard is learning exactly what that purpose is.

Here is the deal. I never thought I would be sitting here ready to pour my entire soul on this paper for the entire world to read. However, I owe it to each and every one of you. My story is very real, and I can only hope that it will help you look at life in a completely different way. God has given me a new beginning, and I intend to make the most of it—first and foremost by inspiring and educating everyone I can. If this book touches one person, I will have made a difference. Open your minds and your hearts. My journey will touch lives all over, whether they are cancer related or not. We all have cancers in our lives, and we can rise above and truly turn them around and beat them. Our hardships are only as big as we make them. In this complicated world we live in today, we have to believe and know God will see us through. My hopes are that after reading this book you will be stronger and more spiritual than you ever thought possible. Just remember: God never puts more on us than we can truly handle. I am living proof.

CHAPTER TWO

The first thing I want to say is this is not a "Why me?" book. The last eleven months have been brutally honest. Everything I have gone through has only made the path for my life seem so clear. It is so weird that I am sitting in the place I am right at this moment. I have always been the one who didn't like confrontation. Ironically, I feel like my life for the past year has been one big confrontation. I have always been the type to find the good in everything. I have always thought of myself as a fighter. No matter the situation, I am the kind to work my way through it. I have really been through many hardships in my life.

When my parents divorced, I thought my world was ending. I was only sixteen years old and very unsure of why my world as I knew it was crashing before me. To be honest, I think I will never completely get over it. But I fought so hard to put it behind me. I realize that it was all out of my control. Now, I must tell you that I have a very controlling personality. I am a perfectionist, and I want things to be the way I think that they should be. After my parents divorced, I made a promise to myself that my life would be perfect.

I saw what my parents went through, and I swore to myself that would never be me. I wanted the fairy tale. I wanted it all.

At a very young age, being the perfectionist I am, I always took pride in my body and health. It is so strange. For some reason—I don't know why—I was always the one that worried. I always wanted to throw caution to the wind and just do what everyone else did. You know, be the kind of person who rolls with the flow and worries about the consequences later.

In high school, my dear friend Tonya was just what I always wanted to be. Tonya was a cheerleader and was …that girl. You know, the one that all girls wanted to be. I wanted to let my hair down and just be a kid. Tonya was always so good at living in the moment and not letting things scare her. Without her I know I wouldn't have been able to be the teenager I was. Tonya went through a lot losing her mom to cancer when we were only sixteen, and yet she still found a way to soar. Even to this day, I am not that carefree person.

As hard as I try, I really never have been one to let my hair down. As a child I never wanted to do anything that would harm me or my body. I never engaged in drinking or drugs. I can't explain it. I really never understood why I didn't want to do the things normal teenagers did. I really thought something was wrong with me. I was sometimes so insistent on doing the right thing that I would end up staying home alone. When I was growing up my mom was secretary of the church, and she always said, "God gave us one body, and it is our temple." I guess it always stuck with me.

In our house we were raised Christian, and we were always taught to do the right thing. I took it very seriously. If I have one thing, I have a conscience. I have always taken pride in my body and that I have never abused it in any way. I was a very healthy child. Not even a broken bone.

After high school I really got into health and fitness, working at a health club in San Antonio, Texas. I taught classes, and I worked as a personal trainer. I absolutely loved it. I became very in tune with my health after that. I wanted to be in shape, and I wanted to help everyone else get in shape.

I have always been the type of person who thinks of others before me. I have always put others first. I get that honestly. My mom is the same way. It was never about her. It was always about me and my sister, Caryn. I have always been close to my mom. I have become the woman I am today because of her. Above anything else, she made sure that we were good people. We didn't have a lot, but we had love. Our house was filled with love. Mom was very godly, and she had a way about her. I have to tell you she was amazing when it came to teaching us the right way. She didn't even have to work at it. It was so natural for her. I am so blessed to have been raised by her. Everything was not always perfect; however, she always knew how to turn any negative into a positive. We always try to treat our bodies with respect. Mom would always say, "It's the only one you will have, so take care of it." I have always tried to follow in line with my mom regarding her outlook on life, spiritually as well as regarding health. I always loved the way she has been her own person. I used to think to myself growing up how much I wanted to be like her. I truly have become her in a lot of ways.

I never knew everything I was about until my journey started. I have discovered more about what I am capable of since all of this began. Sadly I had to go through all of this to realize what I am all about. But at the same time, I am so blessed to have learned how strong I am. My mom has always said, "As long as you include God, it will work out."

When you are young and your parents try to tell you things and guide you, at the time they are just words. You listen to get them to stop. It's like the saying, "In one ear and out the other." You never know the power of words. It's funny because you really don't even remember most of the things that are told to you when you are young until something forces you to remember. It is amazing how all of it comes rushing back. And at that moment you are grasping to remember everything your mom told you. You never imagined you would need those words to get you through every second of every day. I never knew how precious her words would end up being. I hang on to every word. It's crazy, the positions we find ourselves in. You think you have it all figured out at such a young age. You know that invincible feeling. I have come to learn that nobody is invincible. We have to all understand that anything could happen to any of us at any moment.

CHAPTER THREE

Strength within us has to be one of the hardest things to grasp. I have to tell you that our attitude is 99 percent of how we make it up our mountains. If you feel defeated from the beginning then nine times out of ten your opposition, no matter what it is, will win.

I find myself going back to my childhood all the time now. Like all of us, I had a lot of disappointments in my life. However, when something traumatic happens to you, things come back like they happened yesterday. I went back because I wanted to forget my present nightmare. I felt comfort in my memories. They took me to a quiet place. It is amazing what you remember when you want to. Things I thought I never wanted to think about again were giving me such peace. All of a sudden, twenty years didn't seem so long ago. Sad memories suddenly turned into beautiful ones.

Here is the thing: when your future is uncertain, everything gets put into perspective. Remembering the past suddenly made me forget the present. And that was all I wanted to do. I wanted to just get lost. God helped me do that. God helped me relive things I hadn't thought about for years. When your life hangs in the balance, things become so much clearer. I started thinking about everything that led me up to this very moment. It was incredible. It wasn't all good, but I thought that a lot of my experiences throughout my life could somehow help get me through this very dark time. I was looking for strength from anywhere. I started to realize at that very moment that everything I had been through up until then had prepared me for my new battle. Survival! I was desperate to find a way out of this mess.

We never know how strong we are until we are tested. I truly believe that God has a plan for all of us. I know that everything is meant to be. Everyone comes into our lives for a purpose, and it's up to us to learn what that purpose is. I believe in my heart that we all leave lasting impressions on other people, good and bad. I know there is a reason that I have crossed paths with every person I have met. I wanted to look back on all of my life experiences for strength. I started thinking about my life in a completely different way. God doesn't allow us to go through anything without it making us stronger and better people. I knew how strong I had been many times in my past. I went back to those times to gain strength. We have to realize how resilient we are. When you are young, you think that things just happen. It is always about the moment.

We know the Lord. We pray. We ask. We trust. We expect the Lord to step up in our time of need. We live our lives very selfishly on a daily basis. When things are going along and everything falls into place the way we want it, then we don't really think about how close to the Lord we should be. We have this crazy, messed-up way of thinking that the only time we need to get close to God is when adversity comes into our world. It is so weird. I have always been the one to really know how blessed I was. I am not going to sit here and say I have always had the relationship with the Lord that I should; however, I have looked at my life pretty much as picture perfect for as long as I can remember. I have never taken my situation for granted. I could be having a perfect day and stop and think how blessed I was—but at the same time think to myself that this could change in the blink of an eye. I would sometimes scare myself with where my mind would go. I have always had this uneasy feeling about my perfect life. I would always thank God for everything in my life and keep doing the same thing day to day. I would ignore those doubts and keep living in my little world. At the time I would convince myself that I was a paranoid person. I truly was the kind of person who was very grateful for everyone and everything in my life, to the point that I would even make comments to my friends that I needed to savor every moment because it could be gone in an instant.

My dear friend, Vicki, used to tell me how very humble I was for my lifestyle. No matter my situation or my status, I can honestly say I have remained the same. My thought process prepared me for this time in my life. I look back at all the conversations I have had about how blessed I have always been. I have almost in a lot of instances felt guilty. I have made some mistakes in my life, and I am extremely hard on myself. If something bad happens, I want to always put it on myself. Somehow I thought I was to blame. I have done this since I was a child.

There are givers and takers in this world. And, yes, you guessed it: I am a giver. At forty-three, I find myself still trying to fix everything. I desperately need to realize that bad things happen to good people. No matter how hard you try and how perfect you try to be, the fact of the matter is that perfection is simply not reality.

CHAPTER FOUR

So I am going to tell you about my big dose of reality: life is never what it seems. You think you are in control. No matter what our situation is, we somehow think that we have it all together, and if we don't, we pretend that we do. I never thought I would be so out of control. I am an organizer, and I like things the way I like them. I have to say that I never thought I could feel so helpless. I never thought I would be at the mercy of others. You never think that you will have to totally turn everything over to strangers. People you have never met have your life in their hands. I had never felt so helpless in all my life.

January 2010 changed my life and my perspective forever. I went from being a happy mother of two to being scared and uncertain of everything in my life. I have always been very independent and outgoing. I have lived very organized and sure of pretty much everything in my life. Right up until that very moment, my hardest decision was what we were going to have for dinner. And then I found myself having to make decisions that could mean life or death. It is so true when people say, "Live every day as if it's your last because life can change in the blink of an eye."

God will play as big of a role in your life as you allow him to. I believe when God made us, he gave us this ability to feel the changes coming to our lives before they even take place. It is a beautiful gift, and it can dictate our lives. However, we have to pay attention to the feeling and stop trying to make things be the way we want them to be. Things are what they are. We can have all the help in the world—family, friends, and medical support—but only you can truly be your own savior. I know that because the Lord can't be here with us physically every minute; he had to give us his amazing touch to be able to save ourselves. We want every situation to be the way we want it. And when it isn't, we try to ignore it or make it into something it is not. Then, when the outcome of our situation is not what we wanted it to be, we wonder why. We have the gift to control our situations; we have to dig deep and apply our godly instincts.

If I had not done this, I would not be sitting here sharing my story with you. I made a promise to God when I was diagnosed that if he would spare my life, I would share my story and simply inspire people to rely on their God-given gifts to take control of their own battles. We have more say over our situations than we know.

If I listened to others around me at the beginning of this entire process, who knows what would have happened? My family and my best friend literally thought I was losing it. My worry started long before I even found my cancer. It was really strange because I was so healthy at the time. You know how you decide, OK, this is the time I am going to change everything in my life? Hitting forty, you realize you are not getting any younger and things are feeling different inside. I started to have this overwhelming desire to make sure I stayed looking young and healthy no matter my age. I really wanted me to stay me. When

I looked in the mirror, I could tell that things were starting to look different.

I have to say, in a lot of ways, I have amazing genetics. My mom has this amazing olive skin and has never looked her age. I am so blessed to have gotten a little of that.

But it wasn't as much about my appearance as it was my inner self. I felt like the stress in my life started to take a real toll on my body and mind. My husband and I had a lot of changes going on in our lives. In the seventeen years of my marriage, these were the most trying times for us. We were like many other typical families in the world wondering what we were going to do next.

Things had always been secure for us, and suddenly they were all falling apart. Andrew, my husband, had lost his job twice. The economy kept bringing us down. I kept my feelings and insecurities inside. I knew that sharing all of my feelings would complicate things more. I think that by doing this my anxiety kept growing. I tried to keep on keeping on, just like Joel Osteen always says we should.

I do know that God never gives us more than we can handle. During this time I did look up and say, "Really?" I tried not to question him, but it got really hard. Many moves and changes in Andrew's jobs took their toll on our entire family.

I looked at my beautiful young daughter and young son and knew that they depended on me and they were learning from every step I took. They may have been little, but they were very intuitive. More than we ever give them credit for. So I trusted God and kept a smile on my face and found the positive in every moment of every day.

CHAPTER FIVE

I could tell my body was suffering because of all the stressful changes in our lives. I really didn't have much motivation to focus on working out or even eating well for that matter. I knew I needed to get back in the swing of things but couldn't seem to make it happen. Yes, I look back on it now, and I guess I was depressed. I never thought of myself as a depressed person.

At that time the only thing to get excited about were my children. I couldn't get my strength from Andrew. During that time Andrew had to be focused on his career. In the past our relationship had been very stable; however, you can never know how strong your relationship is until it is tested. All the job changes and relocations really had a negative impact on our relationship.

And I say *relationship* because it put a strain on us as a couple as well as our friendship. We had always been friends. Everything else came after that. And that affected the core of our relationship. When that is tainted, everything else starts to fall apart. We both found ourselves in very unfamiliar territory. I felt very vulnerable and alone. Believe me—I know everyone has to deal with things in his or her own way, but some things needs to be dealt with as a couple. I could feel Andrew pulling away more and more.

Most men find their security in financial success, and Andrew was no exception. When that was taken away, he became a different person, someone that was very hard to relate to. He was very withdrawn, and our communication was almost nonexistent. Before the kids, Andrew was literally my entire universe. My best friend Rae could never understand the connection Andrew and I had. I truly thought I had found my soul mate for always.

Andrew and I had our first true obstacle when we finally decided to have children. It was a very hard battle. We tried everything from fertility to Rae taking me to a Chinese doctor. I can honestly say we went through living hell. I wasn't even in my right mind most of the time through the entire fertility process. Five years of agony. Andrew and I prayed about it and agreed we would accept God's plan. Even though my heart was yearning for a baby, God had blessed me with my amazing husband. How was I so lucky?Andrew has always had a strong personality and liked to be in control. I thought it was always because he was making sure our future was stable. I never thought his actions and decisions were anything but taking care of me. I really believed it was for me. We both stood strong in our faith and listened to Pastor Joel Osteen and turned it over to the Lord. I came to the conclusion that if the Lord wanted us to have a baby, we would.

It's funny. I used to tell myself and my family and friends that I had turned it over to God when actually I hadn't. You have to truly give it to him. That is what he wants. God is our savior if we will let him be. We are the ones standing in the way of all the good things we are so deserving of. We have to know that, no matter what, our maker knows what is best for us. I know that more than ever now. I never knew how clear that would be to me so many years later. I am a fixer. I have always wanted everything to be perfect, but that is not what God intends for us. I have always had a less-than-perfect feeling when it comes to me. Never quite worthy of greatness! Not the best student, never a cheerleader, could be a better Christian, and so on. Those feelings have been in me most of my life. Striving for perfection was a constant effort for me. I never felt like I quite measured up.

Conception was one more thing that I was not successful at. It hurt so badly. I can remember I was in a really bad state one Saturday and my dad and Andrew were hunting. My mom was with me, of course! There was never a time she wasn't. I remember that I was sad. I mean, just that feeling of defeat. I was exhausted and had no desire for much of anything. I was very scared for myself. I didn't know how to shake everything I was feeling. So my mom suggested we go to Saturday church at Lakewood to hear Joel Osteen.

I really was not up for it. I tried to make excuses to not go, but my mom really kept pushing, so we went. It was one of those moments when mothers know best. She kept saying that she just felt like we really needed to go. We didn't even really get dressed up. We went in our boots and jeans. It was a very spontaneous decision. I really was not even in the mood to go and try to feel better. You know how when you really just want to be in your own pitiful state? Well, that was where I was. I had tried and tried, and it had gotten me nowhere. My mom is such a beautiful breath of fresh air. She has always said there is a brighter day coming. So we went.

I felt different once we got there. I remember there was a sudden calmness that I felt from the moment we walked in. So if you have ever been to Lakewood, you are going to really know what I am talking about. If you haven't, well, then I am so glad to share this with you. If you have ever seen or heard him speak, it is like he is talking directly to you. When God rained down the gift of inspiration well, Joel Osteen really soaked it up. He makes you feel like you are the only person in the room. It was the night that truly changed my way of thinking. I sat there in disbelief. Joel started to preach about Sarah. About how badly she wanted to have a baby and wasn't able to. I sat on the edge of my seat, and tears in my eyes just fell. I couldn't believe my ears. It was like he had sat down and prepared this message just for me. It was like he knew my desperation. He kept talking about Sarah and about how old she was when she conceived. Wow! I looked at my mom and said, "I get it!" I had thought all this time I had turned it over to God. I truly thought that I had given it all to him, but actually I was still trying to control the situation. I realized that day that it was out of my control. I wanted children so badly; however, I knew right then and there that I would only become a mother if it was God's will. I had such peace within me that I had not felt in so long.

CHAPTER SIX

That night when I left the church, I felt like I had a new start. I had a wonderful life. My support system was incredible. I had my mom, and I can't even put into words what she did for me that night. It was like she knew. She is truly amazing. I had the most amazing best friend in the world. God puts people in our lives for a reason. Rae and I had such a connection from the very beginning. We have been through a lot together, and I couldn't have gotten through this horrible time without her. I can honestly say she never gave up on me. Rae gave me the courage to keep going and never closed the door on becoming a mother. She has held my hand and been right there with me through a lot of things. When I had given up on getting pregnant, she hung in there and convinced me to give it one more try. With all the testing I had gone through, we still had no answers. My kids are truly gifts from God! You have to know that you know that you have handed it over to the Lord. It is the only way. We have choices, but I know from experience that if it is God's will, it will be. Turn it over to him, and you will be amazed at what will happen in your life. My sweet friend Vicki used to always tell me that God is never late! God is always right on time. I see exactly what she was talking about. What we want is not always best for us. If we would learn to live our lives according to that way of thinking, the world would be a much better place. You have to trust. Trust in God and yourself.

CHAPTER SEVEN

Everything happens for a reason. I had the kids exactly when I was supposed to. Living my life up to this point, I have come to know that every event, good or bad, that happens in our life and every choice that we make puts us right where we are meant to be. The bad makes us strong. The good lets us know it's all worth it. All the heartache I went through waiting for my children was worth the heartache. Without them, who knows? After this hard time, I have to say my life was pretty perfect for about six years. My family was perfect, and our world was pretty stable. We were living in a suburb of Dallas, Texas. I had all my family and friends near me. Rae and I had gotten separated for about a year, and then she and Steve finally moved to Dallas from Houston. That was like the last little piece to my puzzle. I was grateful because Rae and I have a bond like no other. My relationship with her has always been very easy. It was a friendship made in heaven. I knew she was special when I met her; however, I didn't know just how special. We became close friends right from the beginning. We had so much in common that we knew it was a friendship brought to us by God.

Rae helped me through a lot early on in our friendship. Trying to have the babies—well, I couldn't done it without her. When I started my journey to have the babies, she was there for me. Always just to give support. She wanted me to do what I thought was best.

One afternoon I had gone to a new doctor to get a second opinion. This was a visit during which I really thought I was going to get some answers. Instead, I found myself in a very frightening situation. I was there all alone and very scared. I was twenty-nine years old and very confused. Now that I am in my forties, it is funny. Twenty-nine is still a baby. Looking back on it, I was very naive. I was there to talk about having a baby, and the visit ended up not being about that at all. Since I was a new patient, she wanted me to have a complete checkup. So we went over all the normal stuff, and then she did a breast exam. Talking the entire way through it, the words she was saying were scaring me. She proceeded to tell me that I had very lumpy breast and lots of these things called fibroids. I had never had anyone tell me that before. The way she said it had me very nervous. So being who I am, I start with all the questions. I remember asking her if that was going to have any bearing on my having children. At that time in my life, that was the only thing on my mind. She said that it had nothing to do with that. She wanted me to go and have a test called a mammogram. I asked her what the test would show. She then proceeded to tell me it would detect if any of the fibroids or lumps that I had were benign or cancerous. And I can remember right at that moment my heart sank and I thought I was going to throw up. I said, "Cancer?" What? The doctor said we needed to make sure before I continued to try to get pregnant.

I knew nothing about cancer except for what little I knew about my mom's mom. My "memaw" passed away from cancer, but I was only eighteen years old and didn't know all the details about her illness. I just knew cancer was a very horrible word and it didn't even run in our family. I knew how much she suffered. It was awful for her and our entire family. I can remember her pain was relentless. Right at that moment, I had never been more frightened in my life. I wanted a test done right away. I knew I wouldn't be able to function until I had the results. I can remember I called Rae at work and told her what the doctor had said. I didn't want to call my mom and worry her. I wanted to go have the test done and then tell her. I remembered all her heartache with my memaw, and I didn't want her to worry until I knew something. I asked Rae to go with me. When I talked to Rae, she immediately calmed me down. I was hysterical! My whole world had changed in an instant. Rae explained that lots of women have these. I can remember to this day the calmness in her voice. It was the voice of reason. She said, "It is nothing, and that is what we are going to prove! " She was so angry about the way the doctor had told me and scared me so badly. I went and got her, and we went back to the hospital. I remember praying the entire way. I kept thinking this just couldn't be. We got there, and I was crying and shaking during the whole process. I will never forget how cold the room was. I didn't know what to expect. When I went into the room, I could not even tell the nurse my name. Rae had to do it all for me. She was my angel that day. I could not have gone back there without her.

There are people in your life that make you stronger. They bring you up, not down. Joel Osteen preaches that those are the people we have to surround ourselves with. I remember taking that gown off and feeling so vulnerable. I had never felt so invaded in my life. I had to tell myself I could do this. When I got in the room, I remember looking at this big machine that took up most of the room. The lights were turned down, and I just had a very eerie feeling. The nurse was so sweet and did it as quickly as she could.

Rae and I are really different in one way. Rae doesn't really worry about things until it is time. I worry before I even have any idea what is going on. We are very different in that aspect. I know I scared Rae because I got so worked up about this whole ordeal.

I was worried before we even got started. After I got dressed, the nurse gave me my checkout papers, looked at me with the most caring look on her face, and said she would rush the results and call me right away. It was a Friday, and she worried about my waiting over the weekend.

We left, and I remember Rae and I thought it was the longest day ever. Now remember this was in 1998 and things were a lot slower back then. So we truly thought it was taking forever. They moved my tests to the front of the line and got them done that day. They called me with the best news I have ever gotten. Everything was perfect. It was only what they called fibroids. They told me that I would probably always be prone to having them. But that was all it was. What a beautiful feeling. I was going to be just fine, and once again I could focus on having a beautiful baby. That was exactly what I did. From that day on, in spite of my happiness that scared never left me. I mean, deep down in my soul, I had this weird uneasy feeling. I prayed about it and asked God to please help me to stop obsessing about it. I wanted so badly to let it go. I got to a place where I finally did just that. I let it go and decided to say it was over. I talked to myself every day and told myself I was fine. I started to think it about it less and less.

CHAPTER EIGHT

I tried to put my fears to rest and didn't think about it much. I focused on Andrew. I have to say I completely put my whole self into my work and Andrew. It had always been just the two of us, and that was OK. I found comfort in just taking care of him. It gave me a purpose. I never want anyone to want for anything. Making Andrew my world was how I defined myself. Not being able to conceive made me feel so much less of a woman. I fell short, and I guess the only way to try to put it behind me was to focus on him and what made him happy. It is like I picked up right where his mom left off. I had no idea what the repercussions for my actions would be later. I was so young, and I wanted self-worth. I guess I felt like my only way to prove myself was to be the wife and person I knew Andrew wanted me to be. From the very beginning, I learned Andrew was a perfectionist. Being his wife in a lot of ways was very stressful. Being perfect is very hard to accomplish day in and day out. I started to believe that God knew that being Andrew's perfect wife was all I could handle at the time. My marriage was the most precious thing to me. I put a lot on myself in the sense of not being able to conceive. I blamed myself and spent every moment of every day trying to make it up to Andrew. I have to say there weren't a lot of things I would have changed about Andrew, but I think if he had a more sensitive side, it might have made my whole breast-cancer scare somewhat easier. Not to mention having trouble conceiving. I desperately wanted him to have a softer side and not to be so rational. He used to tell me I thought with too much emotion. He was all about the practical side of everything. It's funny because at the time I didn't realize the crazy twists and turns our life would eventually take and how important it would be for him to have a little bit of softness within himself. All the things I loved about Andrew I thought would make up for his insensitivity. I thought I had enough for the two of us. I wanted the life we had together so badly that I could overlook some of his stern ways. When you are young, you live in the moment. I especially did simply because that is who I am. It's funny that Andrew and I were as close as we were. He was always so logical. I was anything but logical. I always want the brighter side. I will find the good in anything bad. Andrew was the kind to always say, "It is what it is!"

Andrew's dad was in the military for a good part of Andrew's life. Andrew looked up to his dad with strong respect. Once I met my father-in-law, John, I understood a lot more about how Andrew came to be the person he was. They both are very smart and analytical people but also extremely reserved. It has to be pretty big to get a rise out of either one of them. Natalie, Andrew's mom, was OK with that I think. I thought I was too until our perfect world started to not be so perfect anymore. I really believe that the hard things we have to endure in our lives allow us to reveal the truths not only about ourselves but also about the people we think we know the best. The harder times we go through, the more we truly realize whom we have chosen to share every good and most importantly every bad phase of our life with. When we get married, it is all about the happiness. I was twenty-four years old and I listened to the vows but didn't really hear them. I heard what I wanted to hear. Only the good! Especially me! I am such a positive person that I really didn't think we would have many bad times to come. Everything had always come so easy for Andrew and me. Most everything we touched turned to gold. When you have lived a very blessed life, that is the only road that has been revealed to you. Our road had always been easy. The only road we knew was a road without bumps. I was in for a huge awakening. Andrew really was too.

I had always thought Andrew was the stronger of us. No matter how stern Andrew was about money or anything else in our marriage, it was worth it because I felt secure. I knew he would always take care of me. The security was priceless. I did an OK job of taking care of myself before I met Andrew, but he was great at building our future. Financially he was a wiz. He knew exactly how to take care of us in that aspect. Andrew has always measured his success by his net worth. Right or wrong that is the way he was, and I was all right with that. I thought he was brilliant and invincible. My strong husband ended up not being so strong. To hear him tell the story, he never wavered. I see it completely different. As long as everything went according to plan, he was unbreakable. When things got hard, though, he got introverted. I didn't really realize the devastating effect this would have on me in our years to come.

CHAPTER NINE

So after a while of just living and not really thinking about starting a family, we slowly started to have small conversations about it. I can remember sitting there together and asking each other, "Why us?" We talked about what great parents we would be and what a great life we could provide a child. Trying not to doubt God, we would look around and wonder why others would have a child whom they couldn't even take care of for one reason or another. So our talks got longer and more frequent, and I decided I was ready to take one more journey down the baby road. I yearned for a child from the most high God.

People would ask me, "Why not adopt?" I would say to them I wanted Andrew's child. I felt very strongly concerning adoption. It is an amazing thing for some people, but it wasn't for us. We both agreed. So we continued on living our lives single. I always mean *single* as in no children. Our life was good, but I always felt the void. I wanted to be a mother. I started to think I would try anything to get pregnant. I started to ask anyone and everyone I knew about my options. My best friend Rae found this Chinese doctor and took me there. They ran these tests on me and looked at my eyes. It was very strange. I was willing to do anything. The doctor gave me this horrible black tea. It seriously looked like tar. I wanted a baby so badly I was willing to do anything including drink this horrific tea. I would put all my faith into everything I tried. I just knew the next big idea would work. Neither the tea nor all the other quirky things I tried worked. Trust me: when you're desperate, you will try anything without thinking of any negative consequences. I went to everything thinking it was going to work. I have always had that outlook in all that I do. Nothing worked. Here we were once again at a dead end. Exhausted again, I took a break from it all.

I soon was introduced to a girl who quickly became a friend and come to find out we had similar stories. It took her a long time to conceive. She told me how she became pregnant with her beautiful twins. I was so excited to hear about her in vitro experience and how successful it was. I thought this might be my answer. I got her doctor's name and made an appointment. This doctor was not a specialist of any kind. He was just a gynecologist. She knew him very well, so she trusted him. Since my friend trusted him, so did I. I wanted answers so we could make it happen. So he started me on fertility shots to make me ovulate. Andrew gave them to me at home. I took them for so many days, and then I would wait. The doctor would have me come in to see how well the shots worked and how many eggs I produced. I would go in, and I can remember one month I had about ten follicles. Then I would go back the next day, and they would all be gone. This was huge because at least I knew why I wasn't getting pregnant. I wasn't ovulating. It was an emotional roller coaster. It was a nightmare. I was truly a basket case from all the shots. My hormones were incredibly messed up. The doctor wasn't sure what was happening and why the eggs were diminishing. I came to find out the doctor I was going to had very little knowledge about fertility shots and what that type of medicine could do.

I had no idea, and I was back at square one. I couldn't believe I could get so close but be so far away. We could not figure out why this was happening, and I was getting too exhausted to continue. My body took such a toll through that entire process. Rae begged me to keep my head up and keep trying. I started feeling extremely different and weird. I began to have anxiety and panic attacks. I had never had these feelings before. It was terrible. It got so bad I thought I was losing my mind. Everything scared me. Things that made me nervous before all of this were magnified. I would go into complete panic mode. I was extremely paranoid about everything and everyone.

I confided in Rae, telling her I thought everything was getting to me and that I might be going crazy. I am talking losing my mind. Physically I just didn't feel well. Mentally and physically my entire being felt like it was no longer mine. I can remember there was an entire week I didn't sleep. Not one minute. I couldn't relax at all. Everyone I spoke to kept saying I was depressed. They wanted to treat me for depression. I kept telling my mom and Rae that I was sad but not depressed. I went to several doctors just to have them tell me that nothing was wrong except that I was consumed with having a baby. If I had a dollar for every time someone told me to stop trying, I would be a millionaire. Seriously, I would. If I heard it once, I heard it a million times. "You are way too highly strung, Christi. Let it go, and it will happen." I was told that so much I started to believe it. Psychologically it was so hard, but I knew deep down that there was something physically wrong with me. It was a physical condition that was making me unable to conceive. I wasn't the doctor, and I thought I had done everything I could to get pregnant. I trusted the doctors because that is what you are supposed to do. They have gone to school, and they are educated. They not only all came up with nothing but also almost convinced me that I was *crazy*. I was headed down a very dark and destructive road. I wanted a baby so badly, and I didn't know to whom or where to turn.

CHAPTER TEN

My mom and Rae tried to keep me motivated as much as possible. Suddenly I found every day going by faster and faster. You know how everyone loves to tell you what they think. I know in our lives people want to help and give advice, but sometimes it truly just makes it harder. It seems like when you really want something—I mean really want something—you see it all around you. It's kind of like when you decide to buy a new car and you take a long time to decide what kind. You shop around and finally make up your mind and buy it. You didn't see many of them on the road until you drive yours off the lot, and on the way home, you see more of that car than they had at the dealership.

It's funny because before Andrew and I decided to try for a baby, I never really thought about who had kids and who didn't. I never babysat or really noticed them. I lived my life, my marriage, and my career. That was pretty much it. Then once we decided to start a family, it was everywhere. It seemed to come easy for most. It just happened for all of my friends and family. The more people I knew with families, the harder I was on myself. Christmastime was the worst. We would receive Christmas card after Christmas card with everyone's children on them. I would tell myself that it wasn't going to bother me this year, but every year got harder and harder.

Mom and Rae went through every emotion with me. I expected it with my mom but not with Rae. We had only been friends for a short while. It's one of those godly things. I know that God puts people in our life for a reason. I truly believe Rae was my angel. She has always been as good of a friend to me as I was to her. Rae always had a way of making lemonade out of lemons. Rae wanted me to have children as bad as I wanted to have them. Our friendship grew very quickly, and it was solid from the very beginning. There were a lot of days when I was going through my lows and couldn't have made it without her. Truly I couldn't have. I think she prayed and thought about my becoming a mother as much as I did. There were many days I wanted to throw in the towel. I think the best thing about our friendship was that she followed my lead. On the days I was tired and weak, she knew just what to say and when. On my strong days, she built me higher. If you look at your life and all the relationships you have in it, there are probably one or two people you can actually relate to. We look to people sometimes when we are desperate for support that isn't necessarily a positive influence. In fact, it may only add fuel to the fire. In my situation, I was desperate, and before I had Rae, I would tend to try to get advice from anybody that would listen. When people don't know your situation in its entirety, it truly can make or break you. Desperation is a very vulnerable place to be. You find yourself listening and doing things you never thought possible.

I was still back at square one: not pregnant and wondering why once again. I would be lying if I said I didn't question God. I tried so hard to understand, but at night when it was dark and quiet, those thoughts would come in my mind. Why me? What is wrong with me? It's one of those things I felt guilty to question, but I wanted answers. I really began to think this might all be happening because I doubted the Lord. I was raised to believe that you don't question. My mom raised us knowing that ultimately we aren't in control. Try hard and then turn it over. It was a hard thing to grasp that what I wanted for myself wasn't always the best thing for me. Timing is everything. It's not about our timing; it is about God's perfect timing. God is never early or late; he is always right on time. I never really realized that timing dictates our entire path in life. If one thing, one split second, were changed in our past, our entire present would be nonexistent.

CHAPTER ELEVEN

In my exhausted state, I wanted to slow down and not think anymore. I mean I just wanted to think about little things again. I felt defeated, and I was tired of it all. I told my mom and Rae that I thought I was ready to move on for good. I looked at my life for what it was at that very moment. I had a great career and solid marriage and my health. So I needed to be thankful and just live.

About the time I started to get comfortable with my decision, Rae called and said we should talk. I could tell she was very eager but, a little apprehensive. I know she didn't want to stir things up again but truly wanted me to explore one more option. So Rae suggested I go to one more doctor. I was completely exhausted. The thought of going through it again was very overwhelming and scary. I was worried about being disappointed all over again. However, I remembered that night at church, and I pushed forward. I knew God would be right there to catch me if I fell. So I went with my Mom and Rae to her doctor.

Dr. Thompson was a very strong soul. You just know right away he is in control. I knew he really cared about me and my situation.

After that visit, my outlook was completely different. I was ready! He ran some basic tests that had not been ordered through all the madness. They were simple routine tests. He did a laparoscopy on me. It is a very simple procedure that Dr. Thompson wanted to explore. The day I had it done, my mom, Rae, and Andrew were there. They have to put you under for the procedure. When I woke up, I remember lying there still out of it and hearing Rae first.

She told me, "They did it! You are going to have a baby!"

I will never forget her voice. I could feel the tears falling. I was so out of it, but you'd better believe I heard that. They explained to me I had a condition called endometriosis. It is common in women. Dr. Thompson let us know I had a severe case of it. If I had gone even a few more months, I wouldn't have been able to have children. They would have had to do a hysterectomy on me. And my dream of having children would have been just that: a dream!

If I hadn't listened to Rae, and kept my dream alive, it would have all been just a thought. Children wouldn't have become a reality. I made wanting to be a mother a living, breathing reality. God kept this feeling in me as I climbed uphill, and it would pay off. Somehow, someway, it would matter if I just didn't give up. If I would believe in the unknown, I would see what God sees. And it happened just like that. We always want to see to believe. We want guarantees in life. If we have to go through hell on earth, then we want a fairy-tale ending. Well, I can tell you that most of us know that just isn't how it works. The thing that we have to know and hang on to is that fighting the fight makes us stronger. It's not our stories but, God's storybook for our life. I have to say he was right on with this one. My children were born at just the right moment in my life. It was absolutely perfect timing. I couldn't have written a better ending for my story. The outcome could have been as bad as the entire journey I went through to have children. Through never giving up, it happened for me. I became so strong I actually never thought I could possibly be any stronger. It is much better that we have no idea what we are headed for. God has put us here on earth and has a plan for us, but it's up to us to choose our path. We have choices every day and paths that come our way, and God has given us the power to make choices, right or wrong, to make our successes and our failures. I know he is always right there to guide, but ultimately we make our choices and have to live with them. God gave me the instinct to keep going! McKynna and McGraw are living proof of my dedication. It was worth every bit of my pain and suffering. I would not know how a lot of my decisions would affect my future until way later in my life. It is truly a blessing that we have no idea what our future is and what lies ahead for us. We would never evolve and take chances if we did. I would probably not have had my two beautiful children. If I had known then what I know now, well, my outcome certainly would have changed.

All of the things we have now in the medical world to help us through and prevent things from progressing in the wrong direction are unspeakable. The opportunities we have with medicine these days for the good and for the bad are way bigger than I ever thought possible. I ask myself a lot of questions since my cancer experience. I can't believe the need for all of the different tests and medicine we have today. We have so much more than we had even ten years ago, and it's not even close to being enough. What was available to me saved my life. My team of physicians and all that was available to them are why I am able to share my story. You see, as you read my survival story, you will realize that praying and finding the right doctors is the only way to make it through. What I have found is just because people have gone to college and received doctor degrees, it doesn't mean they are true healers. I can honestly tell you I didn't get it right the first doctor I went to and it could have cost me my life. There is more than one element to being healed. You have to have your inner God, and you have your outer God. Your inner God is in your soul. It's a feeling that everyone is born with. We all have a strong feeling deep down when the

Lord is speaking to us. I mean stronger than anything you have ever felt. It will save you but only if you listen to it. Acknowledging it is the hardest part. Allowing yourself to listen to it makes you realize there is something really wrong. Having said that, when you listen hard enough, it gives you the path to follow. You then realize what it takes to make it. The outer God that I spoke of is listening to the inner God that guides you to the godly people and godly places you will need along the way in order to fight the fight and *win*!

CHAPTER TWELVE

Things had not been going as smooth as they normally did in my life. I had been so blessed up until those recent times in my marriage and life. Things had come so easily and I never really wanted for much. We were living in Lexington, Kentucky. Andrew had bought us the house of our dreams, we had our two babies, and his job at this point was a dream position. We thought we had finally made it. It wasn't Texas, but it was beautiful and we were all relatively happy.

We were settling in, and things were going normally. We became close to the builder and his wife, Gloria, fairly quickly. I was so blessed to have her because Andrew traveled with his work a lot. During this time I was able to build a wonderful friendship with Gloria. I came to know she was a loving and beautiful Christian person. I knew that I wanted and needed to get closer to the Lord, and she started to help me do that right away. I have always been a dedicated Christian and had gone to church most of my life. Andrew and I would watch Joel Osteen and get our message through him. Wasn't sure why at this particular time in my life, but

I listened to my inner voice and got involved in a women's Bible study that Gloria told me about. It was on Wednesday nights, and it was pretty involved. When I started the class, I remember thinking how much better and how much closer to God I was feeling. I felt scared and lonely often, but the class helped me feel more at ease. You see, I had always lived very close to my mom, and when I was living in Kentucky, she was very far. My mom still lived in Texas along with my really good friend Vicki and my best friend Rae. It was different starting over in a strange place. I remember feeling very uneasy daily. I had never felt like that. I would wake up feeling something wasn't right. I could never put my finger on it. I would pray and ask God to make me comfortable and show me the way. We had friends there, but it wasn't the same. I missed my family.

I couldn't really talk to Andrew because he had his own things to deal with. I never felt like I could show weakness to him. I was supposed to be strong and deal with things. I can honestly say I never told Andrew a lot of things that scared me or worried me. We grew up in two completely different backgrounds, and we had different ways of dealing with things. I never knew how much that would matter until our lives were turned upside down. The "opposites attract" thing only takes you so far! I think being opposite is good in some ways but very difficult in others. I am a giver and a very warmhearted person. Andrew is a very structured person. In Andrew's eyes, the only way to look at a situation is with facts. There isn't room for feelings and what-ifs. My glass has always been half-full, and his has been half-empty. And I guess that is all right in everyday life, but in a life-and-death situation, it's not. When your life is on the line, you have to know your glass is half-full. Living in a what-if world could perhaps be the only way to get you through your death trap.

I prayed my way through my days. It was the only thing other than my children that got me through. I kept saying to myself every day that it would get better. I started to feel better and better until I started to see Andrew decline. I didn't really know what was up but just knew he wasn't right. I could tell he was slipping and was extremely withdrawn. It was more than normal. He finally came to me and let me know that things weren't good with the company and he was very worried. And before we knew it, he was out of a job. I remember asking God at that moment, "What next?" If I can tell you anything, never ask that question.

CHAPTER THIRTEEN

Andrew went through a really hard time. I had never seen him so vulnerable. We had an enormous house payment and bills and nothing coming in. I put things in motion and went back to work. I was there for him every step of the way. I did everything to make Andrew know we were going to get through this. I couldn't help but know this was another learning curve. I knew the Lord would see us through.

My mom and I started looking for another position for Andrew. So all Andrew and I could do was pick ourselves up and figure it out. You do what you have to. I am not the kind of girl who just lies down, so I didn't. Andrew wasn't himself for a while, but I hoped every day my attitude would catch on. My mom called one day and gave us a lead on a VP position at a company that sounded pretty good. Andrew ended up knowing a guy he had worked with back in their Houston Fitness days. I had a really good feeling about it, and I was very encouraging. It didn't pay as well, and let's just say Andrew was less than enthusiastic. It was a start for him to get back on the map. He went up against several candidates and stiff competition. By the grace of God, he landed the VP spot. It was less money, but I don't think I have been more proud of him. It wasn't what he wanted, but he went for it and made the best of it. We had to look at this as a new adventure once again.

I have to say focusing on Andrew took all thoughts off me if anything. I still had some unexplained worries, but they seemed to be put away. It was a good feeling to think about something and not obsess about what was going on with me. Along with his new position came an entirely new set of problems. Andrew's territory was completely different. We were going to have to move to either Indianapolis or Raleigh-Durham. Since I can move anywhere, being a flight attendant for Southwest Airlines, both were all right. We were really hoping for Raleigh-Durham because it was south. Being from Texas we wanted to go back south! It was warmer. We really kind of got excited about the move and were making plans to sell our house and look for a new place. I have a good friend that lives in Charlotte, and I called her right away. I filled her in, and she gave me so much information. I was so happy, and it all sounded great.

Our biggest issue was going to be selling our dream home in a recession. Really! We never sat down and discussed our finances. He did it all.

So when it came to relocating and deciding on selling our house, it was all him. I didn't want to be involved in the decision making because I didn't want to be blamed for any bad outcome. I knew if I let him make the decisions, it couldn't come back on me. I was always nervous enough with my own responsibilities where Andrew was concerned. I didn't need more on my plate.

We got word that we were going to have to live in Indianapolis. We both were very disappointed. We had our hearts set on Raleigh-Durham, and here was another blow. We had to agree we would go because Andrew needed a job. So he accepted, and we had to make our plans.

I was so disappointed. I knew nothing about Indiana, and I wasn't prepared for it. I had friends close to Raleigh, and I felt comfortable with that move. I can remember that night when I went to bed I asked God, "Can you tell me why Indiana?" I asked him to give me comfort and a sign as to why we had to go to a place that was colder than where I was and that I knew nothing about. I told God I was so very thankful for the job and I appreciated him so very much for taking us in his arms and making it happen for us once again. I felt blessed and scared all at the same time. I tried not to be selfish, but I know that God felt my true feelings. He knew my heart, and I felt extremely guilty. I should have been on my knees thanking him for the opportunity and for really saving us from disaster. Andrew was in a downward spiral, and without God I can tell you our outcome would have been devastating. My love for the Lord was just going to have to get us through this.

I was ready to start down a road with fewer potholes. I mean I know we are always going to travel roads with ups, downs, and bumps, but I felt like we were on a road full of potholes and with a cliff at the end of it. So I told God if moving to Indiana was what we were meant to do, I would do it. I asked him for his guidance and strength for a smooth transition for all of us, especially the kids. McGraw was still so little that it wouldn't have the same effect on him as it would McKynna. Without a doubt she has been the one the most affected by everything that has happened up to this point. We all don't realize what stability really does for children. Even when they are five or six, too many changes can have a negative effect on them for the rest of their lives. I saw it happening to her, but at that point all I could do was ask the Lord to guide us and show us the way. I loved her and did what I thought was best. Andrew never really realized what was happening with McKynna. I didn't really talk about it and tried to handle it on my own. I didn't want to make things harder for Andrew than they already were.

CHAPTER FOURTEEN

We started to reduce our expenses and save money because Andrew would be making a lot less and we needed to adjust our lifestyle somewhat. Although I have to say we hadn't been spending big since the purchase of our home in Kentucky. With a house payment of that size, we would go through our savings very quickly, and that gave Andrew bad anxiety.

Andrew was so stressed, and I could see it more and more. When we talked about listing the house, he insisted on selling our house by owner only. I was extremely concerned about splitting our family, and he seemed to be concerned with saving money. I didn't say anything and just went along with it in the beginning. I know he was desperate to get what we had in the house back out of it. Remember this was in the worst economy that we had seen in years. The housing market had hit rock bottom.

Andrew had to go to training and meet his team as well as get settled at his new company. I held everything together at home, and it seemed like we were both on the same page. I stayed in Lexington and held everything down at the house with the kids. I thought that once he got back from Florida, he might decide to go ahead and list it with a realtor, but he was more insistent on selling it on our own more than ever. He let me know that he wasn't going to be making the same money and we couldn't afford to list it. So the plan was he was going to go on to Indiana, work during the week, and come home on the weekends. I would stay behind until we sold the house, and then we would all move together permanently. I really wanted to list the house because I knew it would sell quicker. I felt with everything going on it was best to just do what I always did and support Andrew in his decision. Andrew started traveling to and from Indiana. It wasn't extremely far, but we were still apart once again. We spent time together as much as we could between Kentucky and Indiana. It was getting really hard, and I was starting to feel very insecure about our situation. I hated being away from Andrew, and so did the kids. I started getting all of those horrible feelings. You know those evil thoughts. You take your imagination to a completely different level. Andrew could tell I was wearing thin but still insisted we try to sell the house ourselves. I became lonely and very depressed. Andrew was out working and meeting new people, and I was home in Kentucky with the kids and keeping up that big house. Always making sure it was ready to show at a moment's notice. I missed Andrew so much and could feel myself slipping. I couldn't put my finger on it, and I couldn't come out of my funk. Rae and my mom were beginning to worry about me.

CHAPTER FIFTEEN

Before this point in my life, it was simple to let things roll off my back and to put a smile on my face. Somehow it was a lot harder for me now. I struggled to get through the day and not let the kids know how much I was hurting. Things had changed so much once again. I couldn't believe we truly were here. At that time we were actually living separate lives. I was ready to bring our family back together once again. In our relationship I was never really jealous and never worried about Andrew ever meeting someone and being unfaithful. He had never really given me a reason and was always very mindful of it. When moving to Lexington, he did everything he could to get us together. Somehow I felt like it had changed somewhat. I think the pressures of everything were starting to cloud his judgment. I wanted to go and be with him. I had all the responsibility for the kids on my own. I was lonely and stressed, and I missed my husband.

I went to Indianapolis one weekend and was able to see where he was sleeping and what his world was about. We were always such a unit it was so weird to experience his life that at the moment I really wasn't a part of. We got to the hotel, checked in, and got settled. We decided to get dinner, and I remember thinking how weird it felt. I had never felt so distant from him. I could tell that because he had not been around the kids much lately, they got on his nerves easier than usual. I felt very nervous the entire time I was there. I knew when I pulled out to go back to Kentucky, I needed to make the move. We all needed to be together to survive. Andrew and I had come too far to lose sight of what we had built together. He wasn't himself, and I knew at that moment that I wasn't strong enough to put up a fight. I had no idea what was going on with me. I really did not know why. I had so much fear built up in me and could not shake it.

The next weekend, he came home. I remember being very defensive and couldn't believe how defensive I was. He told me he had met these girls in one of his clubs and they made a deal and he was going to start selling this new health product, MonaVie. I felt so scared and angry all at the same time. I started to drill him about the entire situation. Andrew let me know that he wanted me to talk to one of the girls and said I would really like her. I will say that I was thinking to myself already that I did not like her. It was so unlike me, but I could not help myself. His first night back wasn't so great. I waited until the next morning to let him know that I was tired of being apart and wanted to move to the hotel with him. I had a terrible feeling and couldn't think of anything else. I think he really tried to include me in his new venture with MonaVie. Andrew gave the girl with MonaVie my number. He was really pushing for me to start taking the product. I was really mad initially. I felt extremely jealous and did not want any part of it. It was like he had a life that I wasn't a part of. I had never experienced these feelings before. We had always been connected in every way, so I felt threatened. I didn't know anything about Indianapolis or what was there. Andrew wanted me to talk to this girl he had met regarding the product. I hadn't been myself lately, and I had a lot of anxiety. I couldn't put my finger on it and why I was feeling so separated. Everything that had been going on was so overwhelming, and I wanted to think it was because our family was disconnected. I knew that I wanted to get to Indy as soon as we could.

Out of sheer desperation, I made the decision to call the girl with MonaVie, to learn about the product and to see what she was all about. I ended up having a great conversation with her and learning a lot about my health and that it might be able to get me through my rough spot. I had not been sleeping well, and I just wasn't myself. So somehow I thought this might be my answer to feel better. I expressed to Andrew once again that I wanted our family back together and would be willing to live in the hotel until we sold our house. I thought moving the kids into the hotel was scary, but you do what you have to do. My family was my number-one priority, and I thought keeping us together was the most important thing. So Andrew and I discussed it and decided to make a go of it. I was going to leave my beautiful dream home and move the kids into the Springhill Suites.

CHAPTER SIXTEEN

Once again Andrew had to work, so my mom came in and we packed what we needed for the meantime and what we could fit in a hotel room. I had to pick and choose what was most important and what the kids thought was most important. Trying to explain to them that we had to leave our home and move to this little room was very difficult. They couldn't understand why they couldn't bring their entire room. It broke my heart. I know it seems small, but to them it was all their prize possessions. Their toys and their environment kept them safe. It was an ongoing process convincing them that we would come back and get the rest of their things.

I remember sitting on McKynna's bed in disbelief that all of this was actually happening and that we were going again. McGraw was still young enough that I could make do with him. McKynna was old enough to really feel it. She was affected the most by everything that had happened to us. She was the one that would suffer the most from all of our decisions, and I had no idea this would just be the beginning. Moving again would appear to be the least of my worries.

I would ask myself all the time, "Why Indianapolis?" I knew Andrew had to do what he had to do, but I wanted so badly to say I didn't want to go there. I had started to get used to Kentucky, and in the blink of an eye, I was moving to Indiana. Not to mention that it was an even colder state than Kentucky! I knew nothing about the Midwest, and frankly I was OK with that. I did what I had to do and made the move.

I prayed a lot about it. I know you are not supposed to ask God why, but I would. I kept asking him to reveal the reason he wanted us to be there. I knew there was one and he just hadn't shown it to me yet.

We moved at the end of the summer. I wanted to move to get McKynna in school. I already had so much guilt where she was concerned. When we moved her to Kentucky her kindergarten year, her schooling suffered terribly. McKynna came from a dream school in Dallas. I walked her to school every day, and her teachers were amazing. McKynna was just a small child, and I am amazed that she can remember everything about living in Dallas to this day. It was her safe haven. After we left there, her life was anything but normal. The guilt I had from all of it was overwhelming. I have tried to make that up to her every day of her life. Here I was moving her again. I tried to plan the move so we could put her in right when school was starting and she could feel like she belonged and just be normal. We got in the hotel and settled in the best we could. It was such a small room, and I went and got buckets for clothes and toys to try to organize the best I could.

Throughout this entire process, I started to learn more about Andrew. There was a lot about Andrew I really didn't know. When things are going well for a family, it's all good. I was so blessed to have had so many years without one problem. When things started to get difficult, I started to see a husband I didn't really know. We were so close, but I was so naive to think I knew it all. In our marriage I always wanted to be the perfect wife. The more I was around Andrew again, the more I realized he wasn't the same person and neither was I. But I married for better or for worse and in sickness and in health, and I was about to find out the true meaning of the vows I took in front of God and everyone we knew all those years ago. Moving to Indiana seemed to be the only way for our family to survive. All of a sudden, I knew I had to step up and be the positive in our home to save it. I had to commit to myself and to God that I would see this through to the end. Once again living in a new place and a hotel; I had my work cut out for me. I wanted my family intact, so we moved and started our new adventure in Indiana.

CHAPTER SEVENTEEN

I felt like I had to get to know my husband and his world all over again. I felt very out of place. We were trying to get settled in a hotel room and make it our home. I mean, it was no bigger than a minute. Let me just say it wasn't a huge suite. I asked God to keep reminding me the most important thing was our being together.

I started to get to know people around the hotel and familiarize myself with the area. I really liked the city. It felt like what we were used to. We moved at the end of the summer, so the weather was pleasant. I could still feel the tension with Andrew because of his job and the fact that we still hadn't sold the Kentucky home. It was all so stressful. I enrolled McKynna in her school and McGraw in his preschool. I was very excited because the people in Indy welcomed us with open arms. As soon as we got there, I started making relationships with people who I had no idea would play a major part in my life as well as the kids'.

I started to feel relaxed and see this as the new beginning we needed so desperately. We looked at homes, and it really made me excited to think we could put some roots down and be happy once again. It had been so long since I felt happiness that I was desperate for it.

It was very strange living in the hotel. The people God had surrounded us with were our angels. They were all so amazing and accommodating. The kids felt so special. At the time they were really into watching *The Suite Life of Zack and Cody*. They used to tease the kids that they were the Zack and Cody of our hotel. They loved it and thought they were famous. I hated the thought of living in a hotel, but we were together. I had to always watch the kids like I never believed I would. We never had privacy, and we were always with strangers. The kids had to learn at a very young age that we couldn't trust anyone. I had to explain over and over that just because people were nice didn't mean they were family. That was really hard to make a four- and six-year-old understand. I couldn't leave them alone for a second. I couldn't turn my head for a moment. There was never a time when they weren't with me every second.

From the very beginning, I liked everyone we met, but there was one special person God led to me. It was like he put me in that hotel for the simple reason of meeting Catherine. I don't even know where to start with Catherine. This woman, the manager of housekeeping at our hotel, would become one of the most important people in my life to this date. She would be one of the people in my life that would play a major role in the long journey that I traveled in a short period of time. Catherine has this special gift. It is a softness that I have never known from anyone else. We became friends and started talking daily. It was a very bright spot in my day. I remember going downstairs in the morning when the kids were still asleep and getting my coffee. I still think about how excited I was to see her and how I was drawn to her. I wanted to hear her stories and experiences. She was incredible. A woman coming here from the Dominican Republic and making a living here was so inspirational to me. So we became very close very quickly. When I went to bed every night, I would thank God for everything in my life, and I especially felt this overwhelming urge to thank him for her. I didn't know why and didn't question it. I simply added her to my nightly prayers. I felt so blessed, and she helped me get through my days at the hotel. I learned from her very quickly that someone else always has it worse. We thank God for what we have and try not to question him. My faith was strong before Catherine, but it grew stronger and stronger through my friendship with her.

I decided to start really trying to take care of myself. I felt depressed a lot of days and knew that diet and exercise were vital at this time in my life. I wasn't sleeping well, as you can imagine, being in a hotel every night. It was tough. I would lie awake at night and watch the kids sleep. I knew how we got there, but it was still like I was living someone else's life. It was just so hard to wrap my brain around the entire thing. I would worry and pray that we would sell the house so we could live like normal people. I wanted to figure out a way to make money and not have to leave the kids. I desperately wanted to make money to help out because Andrew wasn't making the same money by far. One night it came to me. I decided to sell MonaVie.

CHAPTER EIGHTEEN

I had been taking MonaVie for a while, and it had completely transformed my diet and my body. I loved it and thought what better way to make money than by sharing what had helped me so much. I felt so good, and I felt the need to share it with everyone I knew. That is my nature. If I find something great, I want to share and hopefully make a difference in others' lives too. Andrew had been talking about getting really involved in MonaVie, and he really wanted me to meet the people he knew and get started. Andrew is a salesman, and I am simply me. When I love something and believe in it, all I want is to share it.

So I decided to meet with one of the girls he had met, Jillian, and talk to her about an opportunity with MonaVie. We had a good rapport right away. We were both mothers trying to earn a living and not be away from our kids. I liked her, and we had a lot in common, which made it easy for me. I was motivated and knew this was a good choice for me. After our first meeting, I was extremely comfortable with her and super excited—a feeling I hadn't had in a really long time. I thought not only that I could make some money and be home with the kids but also that if I could make this work, Andrew might actually be proud of me and smile a little from time to time. I desperately wanted his approval, and since this was his idea, I thought it was the answer.

I started to meet with Jillian a little more and got myself really familiar with the company. I was so proud of myself and my drive. I had been so depressed and desperate for so long that it felt amazing to be doing something for myself and on my own. Even though it was Andrew's idea, I took it and wanted to make it my own. So I put my heart into my kids, my health, and MonaVie. I made a way when there wasn't one. I lost weight and was so pleased with my results. It all started to come pretty easy. I loved it.

I remember our first MonaVie meeting that Andrew and I attended and how excited I was. I was finally going to get to listen at my first meeting and hear a lot about the company and testimonials. I can remember I felt so great, and I even went out and got a new outfit to wear. I was proud and eager to learn and build my business. I was not prepared to hear and learn about all the hardships people had. I had no idea how many illnesses people were going through and how they were relying on MonaVie to heal them and make them feel better. I can remember this man telling his story about how bad his arthritis was and how MonaVie was his saving grace. The man went on to say that he wouldn't be walking if it hadn't been for MonaVie. It helped people who had anything from heart conditions to obesity.

There was something that happened at the meeting that I will never forget. It was very strange, and I still remember the way I felt to this day. I remember walking into the beautiful center where the meeting was held and looking around at all the different walks of life in that room. It was crazy; all the people in that room and how all of them had a different purpose for being there. I was a little overwhelmed, but not Andrew. As usual he was in his element. I stayed close to him and was just trying to take it all in. He stepped away for a few seconds, and I decided to get a sample at the table. I can remember looking up and noticing this young woman who was standing on the other side of the table. The weirdest feeling came over me, and it wasn't a good one. I don't know why, but I had a small panic attack. It felt like I stood there and stared at her for at least five minutes. I know I made her feel uncomfortable. She was beautiful and young but completely bald. I could tell she was trying to be strong and had her game face on. I had this scared feeling inside me, and I couldn't figure it out. I felt so sad and worried for her. I knew that she was at that meeting fighting for her life. Her purpose in being there was to find that magical cure.

I left and found Andrew. We had a great meeting, but I just couldn't shake how I was feeling. I went home that night, kissed my kids, and got ready for bed, and I had this uncanny urge to brush my hair and stare at it in the mirror. I have to admit my hair was my world, and I kept telling myself how horrible it must be to be going through her illness and have to lose her hair too. I remember thinking how unfair it was. I prayed for her and thought about her until I fell asleep. I can remember not sleeping so well that night and for many nights to come. I couldn't put my finger on it, but I was really nervous. I got really involved in MonaVie and started really introducing it to my family and friends. It was a savior for me. I even started watching my workouts and my diet. It put me into the best shape I had been in in my life. It was a saving grace for me.

CHAPTER NINETEEN

I started getting closer to Jillian, and I was so happy I had some friends. Things were going really well, but all of a sudden, my back really started to bother me. I had never even broken a bone in my life. I was always really healthy. So I figured it was a pulled muscle. I had been working out so hard and lifting weights, so I thought I had done something to my back. Not to mention we were sleeping in a hotel. The beds were not the best. I never complained about them because to be honest I was glad I had a place to sleep and I was with my family. Priorities become very clear later in life. So I rode out the pain for a while and took Advil. I was hoping it would get better, but it wouldn't go away. I talked to Andrew about it, and he said it was probably a pulled muscle, which made me feel a lot better because he said what I had been thinking.

About a month later, I was really starting to worry because my back didn't seem to be getting any better. I started to lose more weight because I was really worried about what it could be. Andrew would ask me about it, and I told him it was fine. It would get better. I didn't work out as much and tried not to pick up McGraw as much, but you know how hard it is. I loved picking up my boy, but I wanted to feel better so I made every effort. I told Andrew it wasn't getting better and asked what I should do. Andrew had been going to this great chiropractor, and he suggested I should go see him. I had never been to one and was a little nervous. I told him I would think about it and I was going to wait and see if maybe it would get better. I was so worried and didn't want to go to doctor. I decided to take things into my own hands and look on the Internet. I had so many unanswered questions. One night in the hotel room I decided to look up lower-back pain. Let me just say that really wasn't the thing to do. Instead of helping myself, I only made things so much worse. I got on there and read and read until I had so much anxiety I thought I was going to crawl out of my skin. It was awful. Everything I read sent me into a complete tailspin. I couldn't eat or sleep. I was so worried. Everything I read pointed to my having ovarian cancer. I tried to find something else that all my symptoms sounded like, but it all pointed to ovarian cancer. The more I read, the more I fell into this black hole. I was convinced I had it, and I knew I had waited so long there was no telling how far along it was.

My mind was so messed up from all that I read I didn't know what to do or whom to talk to. I knew if I went to Andrew, he would have taken me seriously. Andrew was not the kind to comfort me, saying all was fine. I didn't want him to know that I even looked on the Internet. I was feeling bad enough and didn't want to be lectured. I was looking for anyone to tell me it was fine and not judge me. So I finally told my mom what I had done. I cried and let her know everything I found on the Internet. She was the amazing mother and told me of course I didn't have anything close to that. I love her, and she really made me feel better but only for a short time. I wanted to feel better so badly, and I did for a little bit. The Internet is good for a lot of things and evil for even more. I mean *evil*! When I was going through it and reading all of the stuff on cancer, it was so scary and misleading it was unreal. It has a way of pulling you in and taking your mind over completely. I not only did not find the answers but was also turned into a completely paranoid person. I was convinced and not really capable of listening to reason from anyone, including my mom. I felt myself slipping and not being able to function on a daily basis. I had made a bad situation worse. Taking things into my own hands was not the thing I should have done. So I was left with more unanswered questions and a lot more anxiety. You can't always trust what you read on the internet. I asked God to please help me to stop obsessing about it. I wanted so badly to let it go. I got to a place that I finally did just that. I let it go and decided to say it was over. I talked to myself every day and told myself I was fine. I started to think about it less and less.

CHAPTER TWENTY

It is crazy how when you meet someone you have no idea what role that person will play in your life. All I do know is that everyone that comes into our lives has a purpose. It sometimes is revealed to us in a short period of time, but it could take years. We all have a purpose. All the things we do for people could be life altering. Your decision to help someone could mean something life changing for them and change your life for the better in the process.

Meeting my friend Jillian wasn't just about selling something. In the beginning it was. I met her to learn about something I could sell to make money for my family. Who knew that she would be one of the people who played such a key role in my journey? I have found that nothing in life is by chance. We are meant to be exactly where we are at each moment. Nothing is a mistake. God puts us right where we need to be and with the people we need to be with. We have to look at it that way, or else it could cost us our lives. Not to be dramatic, but it is the way I live my life now. We all have a journey and people who take it with us. God is there and gives us help and resources, but it is up to us to decide how we apply them. The smallest word or act could mean life or death.

When I met Jillian, I truly thought her purpose in my life was to teach me everything she knew about my new business MonaVie, when in fact that wasn't why I met her at all. Jillian would be the one person who would play the most important role in the early detection of my breast cancer. Without her and her kindness, I probably wouldn't be here to tell you my story. So I guess what I am trying to say is never underestimate anyone that comes into your life. He or she could be your angel sent by God. Jillian was such a beautiful person inside and out. One of the most real people I have ever known. The weird part about it is I didn't know her very long before she was really there for me when I needed someone. Andrew was working all the time, and my family was still in Texas. I was in that big new city alone and felt it every day. Jillian was sweet, and we had a lot in common—more than I thought when I met her. MonaVie was such an amazing product, and it really helped me get to know her and special things about her family. Jillian's dad was sick with heart disease, and her mother was sick with cancer. It is funny because we had the same fears for different reasons. We talked a lot through the MonaVie training process, and I realized I could trust her and was extremely comfortable with her.

One evening it was really late and my back was hurting, and everyone was asleep. I was having such a panic attack I couldn't even lie down. I was so worried about my back and why it was hurting, and I explained to Jullian, I had gone on the Internet and tried to find out why my back was hurting me so badly. I had been so worried that my weight had dropped, and I became obsessed about it. I would lie my head down at night and not be able to sleep because I was thinking about my weight loss. I just couldn't shake that there was something terribly wrong with me.

It was awful—so awful that I had decided from all that I read I had ovarian cancer. All from just a small backache. I would say to myself "Seriously, Christi?" I worked out all the time and lifted weights. I picked up the kids all the time. It was just a pulled muscle, but I had convinced myself that I was very ill with ovarian cancer. It was funny because I read about so many cancers and the symptoms of them all, but for some reason ovarian was the one I held on to. I couldn't shake it.

I texted Jillian to see if she was awake and if she could talk for a little while. I was having an attack and couldn't settle down. I hadn't told Jillian about it yet, but I really wanted to tell her in hopes that I would feel better and could rest. I told her all about my fears and the hell I was putting myself through. I loved her because she didn't laugh once or say I was crazy. She told me about her problems with tumors that would come and go. You look at a person and think his or her life is perfect—no worries and stresses—and realize it couldn't be more different. I had no idea the fears she had and was living with daily. It helped for me to know that I wasn't the only one that had such dark thoughts. I was in such a deep, dark place that I didn't think I could get out. I was so consumed with having cancer I couldn't live my life. I had no control over my thoughts. My conversation with Jillian actually eased my mind.

I started to sleep a little more and could cope a little better. I tried so many things to get back on track. I continued to take my MonaVie and work out. It was the only thing that kept me centered. I prayed and asked God every second of every day to hold me and let me know that I was going to be all right. That it really was a simple backache. I found my strength first in the Lord and second in my children.

CHAPTER TWENTY ONE

Andrew on the other hand continued in his own darkness. Our house in Kentucky not selling was taking a toll on him and our marriage. I never spoke to anyone about our hardships in our marriage. It was always thought that we were great and had it all together. I never let anyone know the agony we were going through living in a hotel while trying to sell our big house. I was always very grateful that we had the hotel and the family that we had made there. I would pray that we would sell the home and be able to buy a house and be settled once and for all. I can remember that to fill my days I would go drive through neighborhoods and dream that I was picking out a house and we were going to actually raise the kids there. My prayers and dreams kept me sane. I lived in a dreamworld for a long time and would talk about it to the kids. It was comforting to all of us. All McKynna wanted was to have a room and to have play days again. Her entire life had changed. McGraw was still so little that he didn't really understand how different our life had become.

Our life had become complicated and inconsistent. I can't remember one easy moment through that entire journey. I can describe it in one word: *messy*. I was still fighting with the demons within. The cancer demons were alive and well in my mind. I tried to stay strong, but it was a constant battle. My faith was on the rise, and I leaned on God because I truly felt he was the only thing that could settle me down. I didn't feel like I could go to Andrew and talk to him about all my fears. I already felt so strange and thought I was losing my mind. I really didn't need him to make me feel worse.

One night I finally expressed to Andrew that my back was hurting so bad and asked him what I should do. I started crying and told him I was in a lot of pain and asked if he could think of anything. Andrew once again reminded me to go see his chiropractor. I had never been seen by a chiropractor and had no idea what they were about. I knew they weren't doctors but they knew about the body. So I was open to the idea because I knew they weren't going to test me and scare me. So I decided to go.

Jared was his name, and I liked him right away. Not a judgmental type of person, and he listened to me about what was going on with my back. I can remember when he explained to me what we were going to do to try to get my back healthy again. I liked him, and he was nice to me. The plan was that I would come for adjustments and he would monitor me. The only thing was he wanted to take an x-ray of my back. I will never forget the day he said that. At that very moment, I had a full-blown panic attack. I really did, and I thought I was going to lose it in his office. I hadn't told him anything about my fears or what I thought might be happening to me. I told him I didn't have time for the x-ray but maybe the next visit. He said that was fine but I needed to let him do it the next visit. I agreed and left. I remember sitting in my car and thinking I was never going back. If they did an x-ray, they might find the cancer. I couldn't take that chance. I was so convinced still that I had cancer. You guessed it; I never went back. My back was better, and I didn't want to know the truth. I could deal with the back pain, and I told myself I would take it easy and hope it would continue to heal with the Lord's help. I put my trust in him and asked him to see me through. As time went on, my back seemed to get better and better. I could still feel that it wasn't 100 percent, but I knew God was keeping it at bay. I couldn't shake that cancer feeling away. It had a hold on me and wasn't letting go.

I lived in fear for several months. It was better, so I decided to go to my friend Jillian and ask her for the name of her doctor. I knew it was time, and I had to trust in the Lord to see me through. I called her and said I needed to go get a checkup. My pap and mammogram were long past due, and I wanted to get it done once and for all. I remembered her talking about her doctor and really liking him. I knew how she felt about cancer, and she had such fears that I felt good about using her doctor. Jillian spoke highly of him and trusted him, so I knew I could too. Jillian let me know what a great doctor he was and that he was handsome as well. I thought, laughing, all the more reason to use him. No, really, I felt like it was right coming from Jillian and knowing how highly she spoke of him.

CHAPTER TWENTY TWO

I had talked to Rae about everything and told her that I needed answers, and she agreed. She thought it best to finally get the answers I had been wanting for so long. I got the appointment and couldn't have been happier. I was so thin and frail at the time. I had lost so much weight from worry and lack of sleep. Andrew honestly thought I looked great and had been working out. I literally stopped talking to him about my fears because he didn't take them seriously and he was very busy. It was easier to not discuss it and to deal with it on my own. My mom was still in Dallas, and I didn't have anyone to keep McGraw. I had to bring him with me to the appointment. To be honest, that was the norm for me. It was a rare occasion that I didn't take him with me.

I can remember that first visit like it was yesterday. I was in the waiting room, and it was busy. It was a fairly large office, and of course because he was an ob-gyn, it was full of expecting mommies. I loved being in there with them. It somehow relaxed me and took me back to a place I loved: being pregnant and going on my visits to see my baby in my tummy. But this visit was so very different. I looked around and wished I was back in the time of my pregnancy. Oh, how I wished I was there for other reasons. Sitting in that waiting room and waiting for my turn was truly agonizing. I wanted to be called and called soon before I decided to get up and leave. I talked to my mom on the phone the entire time until it was my turn. My mom is so good like that. Even though she couldn't be there, she made sure she was as close to me as she could be. She had lots of words of encouragement and let me know that all I needed was to trust God and know that all was OK. My mom has the most calming voice. I held it in my head and my heart as I heard my name called. I had to keep it together because I had McGraw with me and didn't want to scare him. I started talking to myself as I was on my way in. I had never talked to myself so loud in my head. I was screaming inside. I told myself to get it together, girl. It's a checkup! Really! You have done this a million times. This is confirmation that I am perfect. I felt like I did the first time I ever went to the gynecologist—seriously—and this time my mom wasn't with me.

I remember going in and the nurse having me change and how the room was so very cold. McGraw was very confused and didn't know why I was changing. He asked me, "Mommy, why you do's dadt?" It made him nervous, but I talked him through it as well as myself. I think having him there was my comfort. So between having God in my soul, my mom in my heart, and my son holding my hand, I could do this. I think it would have been easier if I had been at the doctor who delivered my kids. Instead, I believed that I had ovarian cancer and was coming to a doctor I had never met and who knew absolutely nothing about me while I knew nothing about him. Are you kidding me, Christi? I had to get my answer once and for all. Not to mention my friend Jillian said how beautiful he was.

I felt like I sat on the exam table forever. Dr. Smith finally entered, and for a second it was nice because I was focusing on him and not the fact that I had to tell him I thought I had ovarian cancer. He was a tall and rather large man with very sweet eyes. I have to say he was very nice looking. I was quite taken by him. I immediately felt a calmness come over me.

He introduced himself, and I said, "Hi, I'm Christi, and this is my son McGraw!"

Dr. Smith started into the visit right away. I really wanted to slow it down, but he wanted to know everything about me. The questions seemed to be coming so fast. I remember I was so nervous that I was shaking. I was looking at him as he was talking, but honestly I didn't hear a lot of what he was saying. All of a sudden, I heard him ask what brought me in. Before I could even answer him, I started crying and couldn't compose myself. I could tell he was caught completely off guard. Dr. Smith got up, got me some tissues, and told me to take a deep breath. He was very kind and asked me to tell him the reason for my visit. I told him that I was there because I told him that I thought I had something really badly wrong with me. He asked what I thought I had. I told him in the most vulnerable way I knew how that I thought I had cancer. I was so serious when I told him, and he knew I believed it. Then he did something that I couldn't believe. Sitting on the edge of his counter next to the table, he actually let out a subtle laugh.

I stopped crying in the blink of an eye and looked at him and asked, "Are you laughing at me? If you are, I am going to get dressed and walk right out of here."

Dr. Smith knew how hurt I was and how terrible he made me feel. He immediately said that he wasn't laughing at me. He said the only reason he laughed at all was because he couldn't believe by looking at me that I would think I was anything but healthy. He looked at me and asked me to tell him exactly what kind of cancer I thought I had. I looked at him and was very hesitant to answer him.

He said, "Come on, tell me what you think you have."

At that very moment, I was so scared to actually say it out loud to someone that could find out if in fact I had ovarian cancer. I sat there for a moment.

He said, "What do you think you have?"

I told him, "I think I have ovarian cancer, Dr. Smith. I truly believe with all my being that I have it."

Dr. Smith looked at me and asked, "What makes you think that?"

"What exactly makes you think you have that?"

I told him, "I have had a severe back ache for a long time. I did research on the internet and that one seemed to describe my symptoms. I have literally talked myself into having it, so I need to get some answers once and for all."

Dr. Smith said, "I can see you are worried and really need answers."

Dr. Smith knew how serious I was. He looked at me very sincerely and said, "Christi, I see how concerned you are. After you leave here today, you will know how healthy you really are."

And for the first time in months, I felt like I was going to get answers. Good or bad, I was going to know once and for all what was going on with me. It was such a relief to hear him say that I was going to know how healthy I was. I wiped my tears, pulled it together, and told Dr. Smith that I was ready. I could tell Dr. Smith was very concerned about me. I know in the beginning he thought I was a little off. Not in a bad way, but I could really see that he was concerned about how strongly I felt about having ovarian cancer. To be honest I really think he felt sorry for me. When he looked at me, it was with a genuine sadness for me.

CHAPTER TWENTY THREE

Dr. Smith started every kind of test on me that he could think of. I couldn't believe that he even gave me a sonogram. After they took my blood and gave me a pelvic exam, they advised me that Dr. Smith ordered a sonogram. As much as I was so glad they were testing me so thoroughly, I was terrified—terrified of what they would really find. I had waited months to have the courage to go to the doctor, and now that I was there, I wanted to run. I wanted to run out of there and never look back. I wanted to know, but I didn't.

I waited in the room for what seemed like forever. The tech came to get me and took me back to the room. My life could change from simply walking in and out of that room. McGraw by my side, I was determined to do this. I told myself how very blessed I was that Dr. Smith was the doctor he was. Most doctors would have set up a later appointment time to get the sonogram done but not him. He could tell I couldn't go any longer regardless of the results. The room was very dark, and I felt like a child. I missed my mom and wished so badly she was there holding my hand.

The tech was so nice and looked at me and said, "Are you ready?"

I lay down, and tears started to flow. The table was cold and very uncomfortable, just like I was.

The tech could tell how nervous and scared I was, and she looked at me with the most loving smile and said, "Let's get you started."

I decided to take myself to a beautiful place and not think about where I was. I remembered how excited I was each and every time I had a sonogram done when I was pregnant. I couldn't wait to see my babies. I shut my eyes and thought about McKynna and McGraw and when I saw them on the screen for the first time.

Tears still coming down, I suddenly heard her say, "OK, Christi, you are all done. And let me just say you are as pretty on the inside as you are on the outside."

I could hardly contain myself, and I asked her if that meant I was all right and she had found nothing.

She smiled and said, "That is right. You are perfect."

As you can imagine, I was so very relieved and started to cry happy tears. I couldn't thank her enough. She could tell the level of anxiety I had and gave me a big hug.

"All is good," she said. "You get dressed, and we will walk you back over."

I hadn't felt so much peace since I couldn't remember when. I hugged my baby boy and said, "Mommy is perfect." I said it over and over to him. I picked him up and said, "Mommy is going to be just fine, and our family is too."

I got dressed, walked back over to Dr. Smith's office, and waited for him to return. How things change in the blink of an eye. Before I was so scared for him to come in, and now I couldn't wait for him to come back.

When he walked in, my emotions were high. I looked at him and said, "How can I ever thank you? I don't think you realize what you have done for me and my family."

He looked at me and said, "You are more than welcome, and you are great." It had been a long day and I was ready to go. He let me know the only thing left for me to do was to get my mammogram done and I would be up to date on all my exams.

I asked him if he could set up my mammogram right away so it could all be done. I told him I didn't like getting them done but I had been doing them since I was twenty-nine. He then explained that he needed my past films before we could schedule it, and I said, "OK, I will get them immediately."

I walked out of that office with my son a new woman. I was ready to face the world. All I wanted was to go and pick up McKynna from school and see my children. It was a time to celebrate. I called Andrew and told him that I was perfect and all I needed to do was get a mammogram and I was good to go. I went and picked up McKynna and took the kids to get ice cream. They could tell in an instant that their mommy was back. It is funny because I can remember thinking that sitting there outside at that ice-cream shop with my children was the best. My ice cream honestly somehow tasted better than it ever had. Life was great.

That night I got down on my knees in our hotel room and thanked God for the amazing results I received. It was so funny because it had been so long since I had a good night's sleep, and here I lay awake once more but for very different reasons. I was so happy with excitement and my new outlook on my life that I couldn't rest once more. However, it was much better not being able to sleep for this reason. I looked over at my beautiful children while they slept and thought to myself, no matter our circumstances, I am so very wealthy. I felt like the richest woman in the world. I softly kissed them, looked up, blew a kiss up to God, and said, "I don't know what I would do without you. You did this, and I will be forever grateful."

CHAPTER TWENTY FOUR

It was time to get my mammogram done and out of the way. I called Dallas, where I had gotten my last one done, to see about getting my films sent to me. I was so ready to have it all out of the way. It had been such a long time since I had felt safe and had an extended period of time without anxiety that I was just ready to get it done.

Well, when I called and asked, I didn't get the answer I was looking for. I had no idea it would take so long for them to forward them to me. The nurse on the other end of the phone let me know that it would take at least three to four weeks. I thought, well, if it was going to be that long, I would wait. I hung up and called my mom, who still lived in Dallas, telling her it was going to take at least three weeks and possibly up to four weeks to receive my films. We talked about it, and I told her since I was coming in for the holidays, I would wait and go to my same doctor in Plano, Texas. I loved it there and was very comfortable with the entire facility. I had gone there for years, and that's not to mention McGraw was born there.

I was totally good with waiting until the holidays. I wasn't worried about anything. In fact, I was excited to go back and see everyone. I couldn't wait. I was not excited about my mammogram but knew it had to be done. They knew me and my body. So I was good with waiting. However, it was only October. It was a while to wait but worth it.

It was turning cooler in Indy. It would be our first fall in the North. Indy was a place that had true seasons. It is my most favorite time of year. I love that it is not too cold and not too hot. It is simply just right. I love the falling leaves and the colors that fall brings. I can remember being in Indy at the hotel and waking up, getting my coffee, and talking to Katherine about the change in the weather. I can remember thinking how happy I was to be talking about something other than cancer. I didn't think about it much anymore. I was able to focus on McKynna and McGraw and enjoy my beautiful children. I told Katherine how excited I was to be getting them ready for Halloween. They were still very small, and Halloween was extremely important to them, as it was to me. Other than Christmas, Halloween is my favorite holiday. I love everything about it. I had to figure out how I was going to make it happen. That hotel was not the ideal place to trick-or-treat. In fact, it was out of the question. I knew I was going to have to be creative. My babies were only six and four, and both were so very excited to dress up in their favorite costumes. They thought long and hard, and McKynna was Pocahontas and McGraw was Woody.

It was really weird that year. It was like I noticed everything in such a magnified way. The air was colder and crisper. The leaves were the most amazing colors I have ever seen. I can remember dropping the kids off at school and Andrew already being on his way to work so it was just me once again. I would go and get my favorite pumpkin coffee and drive down this one street in Fishers, Indiana, with the most beautiful fall leaves you have ever set your eyes on. There were many mornings I would take that drive and talk to God out loud and thank him for bringing peace back into my life. I was so settled it was scary. There was just one thing I missed so terribly, and that was my mom. I missed her being with me on those drives. Somehow, talking to her on the phone just wasn't the same. I can honestly say I looked at everything so differently after I found out I was healthy. It was a certain respect I had for everything and everyone in my life. I didn't take one thing or minute for granted. I would travel that road, look at those beautiful leaves, and think that this was the closest I could get to God. It was a feeling like no other. I felt at peace and closer to God than I ever had. It was so weird because it was unlike anything I had ever known. I didn't need to be in a church listening to a sermon. I felt so close to God when I would travel through the trees and the leaves fell so slowly to the road. The air was so crisp. With all that I had been through and how scared I was, I knew this was heaven on earth. I loved every minute of it. It was all so perfect.

CHAPTER TWENTY FIVE

The fact that another month had gone by and I had still not gotten my mammogram was weighing on me a little. I knew I needed to get it done, but the more I thought about it, the more I wanted to go to Dallas and get it done. It was already October, and I was going home for the holidays soon, and I figured I could do it there. I called Dr. Hayes's office and let the nurse know I needed to set up a mammogram during the holidays. I was still so apprehensive about it. Every time I thought about setting it up it sent me into an internal panic. I was fighting myself inside and listening to the devil. It would do it to me every time. The nurse asked me to call her when I knew the exact days I would be in town and she would fit me in. I had been going to Dr. Hayes since before McGraw was born. I felt pretty proud of myself having made that call. It took a lot to take the first step. It is so weird because I think I always feel like I am taking a test and I am going to fail it. Just like when I was in school. It was the same feeling I had when I was a child. Nonetheless, I called and got the ball rolling.

CHAPTER TWENTY SIX

I started getting ready for Halloween and trying to make it as normal as I could. I had no idea where we were going to take the kids trick-or-treating. They were merely babies and deserved their holiday to be special. Living in the hotel was so frustrating, and at times like this, I wished I had stayed in the big house. We would have been away from Andrew, but it would have been so much better for my babies. But I could beat myself up all day, and my decision was still my decision. My mom was going to come in and be with us for Halloween, and I couldn't wait. I think living away from her was probably the worst part of it all. I missed her and her being a part of my life daily. We were best friends and did everything together. It was so hard to do it all without her. I missed her terribly. I was counting down the days.

The weather was changing so quickly. I had no idea how cold it got and how early the temperature change happened. I had to start thinking about the kids and where we were going to take them. My sweet friend Katherine once again came through. Katherine told us that the mall was a great place to take the kids and it would be warm. I called Mom and set it all up. I was so excited about the holidays. I couldn't wait to take the kids home and stay with my mom over Christmas. I was really feeling pretty good and didn't go to my dark place very often. I had planned it all and knew I was going to get my mammogram over Christmas, so I was relieved I had a break from thinking about it. I had a plan, and that at the time was as good as having it done and over. But, for some reason, I still had a lot of bottled-up nervous feelings. I really chalked it up to things being anything but normal. I no longer knew what normal meant. And the most important thing to me was that my babies never worry or suffer. I made sure I was happier and more at peace than ever. It was such a hard time for me. My mom came to Indy for Halloween, and the kids had a blast. It was a great time for them. It wasn't ideal. All that mattered was that our family was together. I talked to God and asked him to remind me every day of my goal. The happiness of my children was what I lived for. Andrew worked so much and was very unhappy in his career. It was nothing like he was used to financially, and we were still trying to sell the big house. It was all so much. October came and went before I knew it.

CHAPTER TWENTY SEVEN

I couldn't believe it was almost Thanksgiving. I hadn't had a good appetite and was still so thin and frail. I thought I was a lot better about the whole cancer thing, but deep inside it was still eating away at me. I tried to keep it at bay. It is so strange because sitting here writing this I get extremely nervous. I can remember trying to not let the devil creep in, bringing all the bad thoughts and weakening me and my faith. I had to trust in God and know that the test proved me to be healthy. I started to thank God for the great test results I was going to receive from my mammogram. I had to think positive and know he was going to hold my hand and lead me.

We went to spend Thanksgiving in Little Rock at Andrew's parents' house. We had gone there for most of our Thanksgivings since I was with Andrew. I wasn't myself, but I had the babies and thought it would take my mind off of the bad thoughts. It was a good holiday, but I just couldn't seem to eat. I wasn't hungry, and trying to make myself eat was only making it worse. I can remember not wanting to go home. I cried a lot while I was there, and Andrew's mom tried to comfort me as much as she could. I can remember how worried she was and how she tried to do everything in her power to keep me busy. Andrew's dad passed away a few years before, and it was from cancer. I didn't tell her a lot of my fears and thoughts, but she knew something was wrong. I can remember sitting and talking to her and how she would talk about Andrew's dad. It seemed like they were married for an eternity. It was so incredibly hard listening to her talk about him and his cancer. It wasn't about me, and I was terrified to talk about his lung cancer. Oddly enough, when I did listen to her, it scared me so bad. But I held on to her words when it was about his cancer. It was so weird. I was so scared of the word *cancer*, and yet I listened to her as if I needed to hear what she was saying for my benefit. After we got back to Indy, it was time to get ready for Christmas.

CHAPTER TWENTY EIGHT

We were still in the hotel, and I knew we weren't going to be getting a tree. I was really sad and depressed because it was my children's prime Santa Claus time and we had no tree to call ours. I cried a lot and couldn't get excited about the holiday much. I know that Santa Claus is not the reason we celebrate the season, but my children deserved to have their childhood and I couldn't help but think they were seriously getting robbed. I was sad, and I felt very much alone.

I took the kids home earlier to be with my parents. I wanted nothing more than to be with my mom and have her tell me she loved me. Her touch was the thing I needed most. I used to say that when God made her, he broke the mold. I can tell you she always knew what to say and exactly when to say it. I can remember walking in and her house feeling so perfect. It looked and smelled just like the North Pole; it was no different from when I was McKynna's age. I was blessed that we had a warm and loving home to take the kids to that year. Christmas 2009 was a good Christmas and a memorable one. It was a Christmas I will never forget on so many levels. I just didn't know on how many levels it would be until the year 2010. That Christmas at my mom's was special and so dear to my heart.

One of my most special friends came to see me one night, and it was a visit I will never forget. I remember it like it was yesterday. Vicki walked in, and the first thing out of her mouth was saying how little I looked. She thought I was small and very frail looking. I think she knew right away that something wasn't right. I was not normal for me by any means. We visited for a long time and talked about our kids. It was so great in that she always makes me feel so safe and so close to God. It's unlike anything I have ever known. It was a miracle that it worked out and I was able to see her. That was a God thing.

I had the best time on our visit home. Our Christmas was so great, and the kids were so happy. It was everything they knew from birth. There was only one problem: the holidays came and went. Before I knew it, I was already on my way back to Indianapolis. I was on my way back without getting my mammogram. I wish I could sit here and tell you that I had a very good reason for not getting it done, but I can't! There is only one reason why I didn't, and that is that I simply put it out of my head. I pretended I didn't need it. I didn't call them. I just want to say before I move forward that having done this could have proved very costly.

So we get home, and the turn of the year happens. Happy New Year! It is 2010! I told myself this was going to be our year. A banner year. The Maynards were going to recover and recover big.

CHAPTER TWENTY NINE

I was of the mind-set that if I had to do it on my own, I would. I was going to be the kind of girl for whom the glass was half-full. Every year as a flight attendant we have to get re-certified for our job. My base was still in Orlando, and we were still living in Indy. I was making plans for my trip there, and I was going to have to spend the night because of the fact that it starts so early in the morning. I had gotten back in the swing of things at the hotel, and the kids were back in school. I was somewhat depressed because I missed my mom terribly. Seeing her during the holidays made it so incredibly hard to leave her in Texas. My mom has a way of making me feel comfortable no matter the situation. I always said it was her special gift. I tried to always keep her spirit with me no matter what I was facing. It was hard because you get so built up and the holidays are busy and there is no downtime. Then I found myself back at home trying to be positive and make the most of our living situation. I initially had my class for Recurrent Training but found that I just couldn't get it together. I rescheduled to a class later in the month. I was happy to put it off and avoid having to travel just yet. It was hard on the kids adjusting after the holidays, especially McGraw.

One night we were in our hotel playing around. McGraw was tickling me, and we were having so much fun. I can remember thinking to myself it didn't matter where you were as long as you were together. It didn't matter that we weren't in the big house because we were a family. Andrew had come home, and I felt so glad that we had some time to enjoy each other. Andrew was playing with McKynna, and I was still playing with McGraw. All of a sudden, McGraw accidentally fell on me and hit the side of my breast. I asked him to stop and told him to settle down a little. I sat up and remember thinking how that hurt and putting my hand on the side of my breast where he landed on it. I was still laughing a little and wanted to cry a little too. When I touched the place where it hurt, it felt a little swollen. I thought it was the way he landed on it. I felt it, and it seemed to be a little swollen—more than the other side. I just thought it was from where he fell on me. I didn't really think anything except that it was going to be really sore. After I got the kids down, I got showered, and we all went to bed. I did lie awake for a while thinking I still needed to get my mammogram. I didn't sleep well that night thinking about it. I had a busy week and knew I needed to make the appointment, but once again my family came first. I had a habit of doing that. No matter what was going on with me, my family came first.

A few weeks went by, and I started to think about my mammogram more and more. I was showering one night and felt that spot again, and it still felt a little more raised than the other side. When I got out, I asked Andrew to feel it and see if he thought it was anything to worry about. I let him know I felt a little difference between the sides but didn't know if it was my imagination. My thoughts can get away from me. I didn't want to jump to conclusions again. My body couldn't take it. He felt it and said it really didn't feel much different. Andrew assured me it was nothing to be worried about. Andrew asked if I had gotten my mammogram yet, and I told him that I had not. He told me to go get it done and it would prove it was nothing. I agreed and tried to put it out of my mind. Of course that was easier said than done. I thought about it for the next few days a lot. I would be lying if I said I didn't obsess about it. All of those horrible memories started to come back, and my fears were taking over again.

One afternoon I was in the lobby area waiting to go pick up the kids, and I was full of anxiety. I didn't even want to stay in my room. I was so scared, and I waited hoping I could see Katherine before I left. I can remember watching the door for her. It is so funny because it's not like she could do anything for me, but she could somehow just make me feel better and calm me down. I needed that so bad. I thought to myself, here we go again. The devil was alive and well and giving me hell once more. And the worst part about it was I was allowing it once again. Finally, Katherine came in, and I felt better as soon as I saw her. I ran up to her and gave her the biggest hug. Katherine knew something was wrong right away. She could tell I had been crying and that I wasn't my normal self. I explained what was going on and what I found. I started to cry and could barely get it out. I will never forget her sincerity and her softness. She took me to a conference room right away and said, "Let's see."

Katherine told me she had those all the time and they were common in all women. I explained to her about my past and how I have always had fibroids. I told her how young I was when I got my first mammogram and that I was aware of what they were. But I also let her know that I felt a little different about this one. I told her I didn't know if I was just being paranoid like last time but I couldn't seem to kick it. We talked about my mammogram, and I let her know I didn't get it done in Texas over the holidays. I was so busy and waited too long for them to get me in. I let her know I had to send off for my last films before they would do one. Then she said, "You should go get your doctor to feel it and see what he thinks."

Katherine didn't seem to think it was anything, and it would give me peace of mind. It sounded like a good idea. I had recurrent training coming up, and I couldn't even concentrate on it. I wanted Dr. Smith to give me his opinion, and maybe I would feel better. I made the appointment and told them I needed someone to check me. They got me in within a few days. Once again I felt better making the appointment and knowing I was going to have Dr. Smith check me. I had grown to have a lot of trust in him after our first visit together. I knew he would know and guide me. It seemed like those days went as slow as Christmas. The unknown was what was so very hard and the fact that I felt so guilty about not having gotten my mammogram done when I was supposed to. I was kicking myself for being so careless and felt like maybe I was being punished for it. I was only a few days away from my recurrent training class and hadn't done any of my assignment. I was so consumed with everything in my life except my job. It is ironic because I couldn't live without my career. It had saved me so many times in my life. I was so very blessed to have it and to have been so involved with Southwest for so many years but put it last. I had to get that homework done and make my reservations for the night. Once I got started, it kind of took my mind off of everything for a little bit. I was so nervous to leave my babies overnight while I attended the class. However, I hoped a night away would do me good.

CHAPTER THIRTY

I finished the assignment and said my good-byes. Before I knew it, I was on a plane headed to my training class in Orlando. I had decided on my trip that I was going to cut all caffeine out of my diet. I wanted to be as healthy as I could. I thought it could make a huge difference in my mammogram. Maybe if I made that little knot in my chest become smaller, I would know it was nothing. I was still so obsessive about it, and I continued to feel it and check it throughout the day. I couldn't even tell you how many times a day I would feel it. I was literally praying every time I felt it that it would be gone. I tired to eat and drink so healthy. I was so scared I was willing to try anything. I cleaned up my diet. I can remember getting all my things together for my class and packing a little snack bag. I decided to drink what was in the training room. They always had water available for us.

I got to my room that night and was so unsettled. I hated being in there alone and couldn't shut my mind down. The room was cold and so quiet. No noise from my kids. I missed my baby boy following me around. I tried so hard not to freak out. I was lying there with so much worry I knew I was going to need help falling asleep. I texted my sweet friend Vicki, and being the prayer warrior she is, I knew she could help me. I loved her so, and she knew everything there was to know about my fears. I let her know I was alone in the hotel room and was feeling very scared. I can remember thinking I needed to feel the power of prayer and I needed to feel it right then. We prayed together, and Vicki helped me to see that I needed to focus on what to do right at that moment. My work had to come first. I had a full day of training and testing, and there wasn't room for my worries. I will never forget what she did for me that night. The way she took charge and prayed with me on the phone was incredible. I felt the calmness I needed to get me through the night. I wasn't even thinking about tomorrow. I had to think of the moment I was in right then. I got off the phone with her and made a promise to myself. I had to get it together and not think about the knot I had found. It was going to be about happiness and Southwest. I can't emphasize enough the power of prayer. I don't know what would have happened that night if she hadn't been there for me. God heard her, and I was blessed that night.

The next morning when I walked into class, I saw some familiar faces, which helped a lot. I sat by a friend of mine I had known for years. I was excited to see her, and it took my mind off of everything for a while. During the course of the day, I noticed she was drinking tea. We started talking about it, and she said she just loved it and was only drinking that. It was a lavender tea and was extremely healthy, and being in my frame of mind, I was curious right away. It was so weird because the very thing I didn't want to think about was the topic of conversation. Breast cancer was brought up and was one of the reasons she was trying to get healthy. She began to tell me her mom had recently passed away from it and she was trying to change her ways. I couldn't believe my ears. My skin started burning, and my anxiety came back with vengeance. I knew I had to keep it together and finish my class. I tried to block out a lot of what she was saying because I would take that information and start to make it about me. I couldn't believe it! I sat next to her in hopes of catching up and talking about fun things in our lives, and instead it was the devil again. It was like I couldn't get away from it. I didn't know what to think. I asked myself over and over in class that day if I sat by her for a reason. Was it a sign?

I finished up the day and left the training room with the sickest feeling. I wanted to get home and see my kids. I felt like a lot of people in my life thought I was borrowing trouble. I was beginning to be labeled a hypochondriac. Sadly that didn't even keep my mind away from bad thoughts. The more I thought about it, the more I really thought it might be a good idea to go get another opinion. Then I started to think about the fact that Dr. Smith hadn't really felt the lump in my chest. I hadn't found it when I went for my checkup. I trusted him, and what better person to consult.

I boarded the plane and couldn't wait to sit down. All my worry and my class made me exhausted. I was so ready to relax. I sat down. I didn't know the crew; they were great. I remember talking to them and letting them know I was on my way home from Recurrent Training. They all had questions about the training as usual. We talked a little bit before boarding, and then I sat and tried to relax. I put my head back, and as the plane took off, I don't know what happened. I just lost it. I sat in my seat, and tears started flowing. I couldn't control myself. I was so scared, and I didn't feel like I could even go home and tell my husband. I didn't want him to see that I was back in that same place once again. I wished so badly I could go home and have a safe place to fall. Instead I was scared about cancer and Andrew finding out I was back in a horrible place. One of the flight attendants came by, gave me some tissues, and asked me if she could help. I thanked her, said no, and let her know I was extremely tired. It was weird, but I could really feel that she cared that I was upset and that she wanted to help me. I sat there a while, and for some weird reason, I decided to get up and go talk to her. I have no idea why I did, but I was just so desperate to feel better. I went up to her galley, and we started talking.

I asked her if she ever had anyone in her family who had breast cancer or who had found a lump in her breast. I will never forget the look on her face. I know she didn't expect for me to ask her that.

She said, "Well, actually, I have." She said she had a lump in a routine mammogram. I can remember my heart was pounding, and I became very anxious when she said that. As she continued to talk about it, she let me know that they biopsied it and it was benign.

I said, "Oh, thank God!"

That was when she said, "What is wrong? I noticed you were upset. Do you know someone that has breast cancer?"

I explained to her that I had found a lump on my left side and I was really worried. I needed to get my mammogram done. She then encouraged me and said I really needed to go and get it looked at. I let her know I was as soon as I got back. I think just talking about it and realizing that women have lumps all the time and they more often end up being nothing did make me feel a little better.

CHAPTER THIRTY ONE

I arrived in Indianapolis, and as crazy as it sounds, I couldn't wait to get back to our home at the Springhill Suites. It was a hotel, but it was where we lived. It was our house. I learned home is where the love is. And my loves were inside the walls of that hotel. When I got there, it was the best feeling ever. I saw my daughter dancing all over the room and my son playing right alongside her. They were so very close then because of our living arrangements. I tried to always look at the positives. It was a very small room but so large and full all at the same time. I love my children with all my heart, and at that moment I knew I had to go get checked. I had to know that I was healthy for them. I had thought long and hard about it, and I decided to go back to Dr. Smith and let him look at me and give me his thoughts.

I called the office the next morning and explained what was going on. I told her I wanted to get in as soon as possible. I had been worried about it for a few weeks and I was sure it was all right but wanted him to check it. The nurse let me know that Dr. Smith was out; however, the other doctor that was taking his patients would be able to see me. I made the appointment and would be going in the next morning. I hung up the phone and felt more scared than I ever. Even more than I felt with my ovarian-cancer scare. I knew this was the right thing. I was so messed up and had to know. I just couldn't shake the anxiety. I tried to put it out of my mind and have a good day. I spent the day with McGraw and waited for McKynna to get out of school. I wanted things to be normal and just not to think about it.

Before I knew it, I was in the doctor's office checking in for my visit. I was scared out of my mind. All of the unknowns were too much to take. I can handle a lot when I know what I am dealing with, but when I don't know what lies ahead, I'm not so strong. Once again I was waiting for my name to be called, and it felt like an eternity. They finally called my name, and I felt like I had been there before. Which I had, but it was very different this time. I actually had something for them to look at to determine if it was reality. I got changed, and I will never forget how long it felt like I was lying on that table. For those of you that have been there, you know what I am talking about. It is a feeling I would never wish on anyone. I knew I couldn't get the mammogram that day, but at least I could talk to a doctor and get a credible opinion. The doctor came in, and it was a woman. I immediately looked and thanked God. I am not sure why, but having another woman there and a professional one at that was a very good thing. We introduced ourselves and then got right into it. She asked me why I was there.

She said, "I have looked at your chart, and you were just here for a full checkup, and it looks like everything was great."

I said yes.

She then asked, "So what is going on now?"

I told her that a few weeks earlier I was playing with my son and he tickled me up on my left side and accidentally hit me on my left breast. "It really didn't hurt, but I naturally put my hand on it as a reflex. When I did, I felt a little something. I can't even explain exactly what I felt. I knew it was different, and I couldn't let it go. It didn't really feel much different if at all from the other side. I don't know why I can't let this go, but I just can't." I told her I was hoping she could help to put my mind at ease. I couldn't believe the next thing that came out of her mouth.

She looked at me and said, "I think you are too young to have breast cancer."

I know I looked at her with a look like a deer in the headlights. I was floored that someone in the medical profession would actually say something like that. You don't have to be a doctor to know that *cancer* doesn't discriminate. I would think that a doctor would be the first one to educate us on that very thing. It can hit anyone at any moment in his or her life. To be honest, the wind blew out of my sail at that very moment. I felt sick thinking to myself, would this exam really have any validity? She then went on to say that she herself was a survivor. I let her know that I wasn't too young to have cancer. I was forty-one years old, and it could be very possible that I have it. At that point she asked me to lie back and let her see what I was talking about. I felt so scared and so sick to my stomach I thought I was going to throw up. I had to have her get me a bucket to keep near me. She felt both sides, making me put my arms up to make sure she got a good feel on both sides. After her exam she let me know that she really didn't feel anything. I told her I had fibroids in the past, and she said it didn't even feel like that. She went on to say that she thought everything was great. I told her I needed a mammogram as I hadn't gotten mine done. She said we should not be stupid and that I needed to get my mammogram. She didn't feel worried in the least. It was *nothing*! Those were her exact words. So I was feeling better. Those were the words I wanted to hear. I was also excited because she was going to give me a script for my mammogram. She said that since I was a little concerned, they would try to get me in ASAP. I was happy and scared all at the same time. I wanted it done but was still so apprehensive about it.

So she said she would put it in right away and they would call me. I have to say after that visit I only felt good for about twenty-four hours. It didn't last long. The weird thing was I was so confident in that office because of Dr. Smith; however, having said that, after that visit I lost a lot of my confidence. I walked away telling myself I could have done that. Really! The only good thing was that they were calling me for my appointment.

A few days went by, and they finally called. It wasn't what I had hoped. Ashley, Dr. Smith's nurse, called and let me know that they still needed my old films from Dallas. I couldn't believe my ears. I let her know that I had found something in my left breast and I really needed to get in. I let Ashley know how worried I was and that it wasn't just a routine mammogram. I let her know I really thought something could be wrong. She went on to say that the doctor who examined me wasn't concerned, but we did need to get one done for my file and to be current. I couldn't believe my ears. I couldn't believe that I really felt something in there and they weren't going to do anything without my records. I hung up the phone, and I was crying and just floored. At that moment my faith in the medical world changed forever. Things are as they are at any given moment. There wasn't one past test that was going to change what they found in my body on that very day. I was so discouraged. I called Dallas again and asked how soon my records could be sent, and again I was told it would be about three to four weeks. It is so weird because when they said that to me again, for some crazy reason, in the pit of my stomach, I felt like that was a death sentence. It sounds completely ridiculous, but I felt it deep in my soul that three to four weeks would end up being detrimental.

In the middle of all of this madness we were told we had to move. My heart sank, and my problems had to be put on hold. So once again I dropped everything about me and had to figure out what we were going to do. We had children, and none of this was their fault. They didn't ask to come here, and it was up to us to see that they were well taken care of. Once again I couldn't believe this was our life. The pressure and the worries were really starting to take a toll. I was so scared that my entire body was burning all over.

I was so scared to tell Andrew since the house in Kentucky was still on the market. I always tried to take care of things on my own. He said it would be fine, and he would take care of it. I hung up the phone so upset and called my mom immediately. I explained to her what was going on and that we were going to have to move to another hotel. I told her Andrew was looking for one right now. Of course, she gave me words of encouragement and told me to turn it over to God. It was all part of a plan, and she let me know she didn't like it, but it was going to be all right and I should let God lead me. I believe wholeheartedly in the power of prayer, but at that moment I needed a miracle.

My mom asked if I had gotten my appointment for my mammogram yet, and I told her what they said. I told her I was going to have to wait now and focus on the kids and getting them settled in a new place, It was a hotel, but we made it our home, and now we had to say good-bye to all the people who had made them feel so comfortable and loved. My heart was breaking for them. I was disappointed, and I know being children they couldn't understand any of what was going on. All McKynna knew was that she had Katherine. Katherine was our family, and we looked forward to her every day. She was a breath of fresh air.

Andrew called and said he found us a new hotel. I thanked God at that very moment that we had a place to go. Mom was still in Dallas, and we had to be out immediately. She offered to help, and I told her it was fine and that I could do it. I loved her for offering, but it was going to be so quick.

Before I knew it, we were all packed up and ready to move on. It sounds crazy, but it was hard to leave there. We had made it our home and had become a family. I had to look at this as an opportunity and hope it would put a little pressure on Andrew to maybe rent us an apartment or some permanent place until we sold the Lexington home. I didn't tell the kids until we were moving on.

I will never forget how hard it was to tell them. I picked them up from school, and as we drove home, we took a different way. They both didn't know where we were going, but they knew it was different. As we pulled in, I explained to them this was our new home. We moved hotels, and this was a better one.

It took a few days, but they settled in all right. Nothing to write home about, but it was a place to live, and God had blessed us once more. We were together. At the end of the day, that was truly all that mattered. It was not the same at all, and I had to adjust. It was such a crazy time, and trying to make it warm and inviting was just not happening. In the meantime, I had been talking to Rae daily, and her Mom wasn't feeling well. In fact, she was very sick, and I was very worried about my best friend. I was so far away from her and not able to help her. All we had was the phone and our voices to comfort one another. And God knows, we did that.

I have to say that even with all that I had going on with the kids, taking care of Andrew, and helping Rae as much as I could from afar, I still couldn't erase the fact that I still had a little something in my left breast that wasn't going away. A few weeks had passed, and I wasn't sleeping for many reasons—but mostly for the very reason that I could not shake the fact that I thought I had breast cancer. I would lie awake all night and think about it. I hadn't ordered my films, and it would still take a long time to get them. Rae was usually my voice of reason and could talk me out of a panic attack. I hadn't been able to talk to her because her mom was so ill. I didn't let Andrew know how scared I was about the situation. He would tell me it was going to be fine.

CHAPTER THIRTY TWO

There was one day I tried to get ahold of Rae, and I couldn't. I talked to my mom at least ten times that day. For some reason my thoughts and worries were taking me over. But I will say it was more than just overthinking. It was an inner voice and feeling in the pit of my stomach that something was terribly wrong. The feeling grew more and more every day.

The next morning I took the kids to school. I had not slept at all the night before. Not a wink. I stayed awake all night with this horrible feeling that wouldn't go away. I felt a sense of desperation. Since both kids were at school and I was alone, I drove around and called my mom. I needed her so very badly, and calling her was my only hope.

I decided that I was so scared that I wanted to go to the emergency room to get it checked. My thought was that I could go in and tell the ER that I had a pain right where the lump was. In the emergency room, to my understanding they have to check out what is wrong, and if you are experiencing pain, they will get to you right away. I was going to do what it took to get in there and have a doctor look at me. I thought they could possibly give me a mammogram right there. So I talked to my mom and let her know what I wanted to do. I knew she was so worried about me and she was dying from not being able to be there with me. I know she was scared and very worried about the fact that I was being irrational. I tried to calm down, but I knew the only way for me to be able to live was to go and let them check it.

So I pulled up in the ER parking lot at the same hospital that Dr. Smith practiced and told my mom I would call her as soon as I was out. I told her to pray for me and that they would be able to give me some answers.

I can honestly tell you I sat in that parking lot for over an hour. I sat there thinking and wondering what was going to happen the minute I walked through those doors. I was absolutely terrified. It was like I wanted to get out and go in but my body was frozen and I couldn't move. I called my friend Vicki and had her pray with me. I needed her to ask God to give me the courage to go in that hospital. I knew if I made myself go in there, I was alone and would have no idea what the outcome would be. If they told me right then and there I had cancer, what would I do? I didn't know if I could handle it on my own. So I sat there until I talked myself out of going in. I was so confused and had so much anxiety I didn't know which way to turn. I knew the kids were going to be out of school soon, and I didn't know how long it would have taken and couldn't take a chance. So I left and drove for a while. I had to think of another doctor to examine me. I had no idea who that was going to be.

When I picked up McGraw from school, I was waiting in the hall with a lot of other parents. I guess I had this terrible look on my face because a mom I was standing next to asked me if I was all right.

I looked at her and said, "Is it that obvious?" I told her I was having a little health scare and I was desperately looking for a doctor.

She then said, "I went through the same thing." She had thyroid cancer, and she loved this doctor. It felt like it was the right thing because the chance of me standing by someone, at that very moment, that had gone through cancer was pretty slim, I would think. I decided to take her advice and call and make an appointment. I was hoping to get in quickly, and I was able to.

They fit me in the very next day. I was so thankful and thought this could be the right doctor that would give me some answers. I needed a second opinion. When I started to analyze everything and how long this had been going on, I got so upset. I could have had this done a long time ago, but I let fear lead my way. Instead of turning it over and allowing God to take care of me, I controlled it once again. I allowed fear to lead me instead of the Lord. I should have learned from the first time, but I didn't. I let the devil right back in, and it overtook me once again.

I went in and met with the doctor, and to be honest it was a waste of my time. He basically told me the same thing. Lay off the caffeine. It didn't feel different than the other side, but we would need to get a mammogram to be certain. He said to get one but he could almost guarantee that it was nothing. I asked him if he could order a mammogram for me, and he said he couldn't without my previous films. I couldn't believe they were saying this once again. I should have known. I told them thank you and I would be calling them to set it up once I got my tests from Texas. I left the office once again without knowing any more than I did when I got there.

I was crying and so frustrated. I didn't know what to do. I could have ordered my films a long time ago, and I should have. But my fears had led me up to this point and literally made me go in circles. It made me so exhausted.

At this point I didn't trust or believe in much. The system was all about the system. I truly didn't feel like the medical system was for me. It was all about them making sure they were covered. I had a lump in my breast, and if they couldn't feel it or see it, I knew deep in my soul it was in there. I had to think of something and fast.

CHAPTER THIRTY THREE

Once again, I went back to the hotel and did all of our nightly things. I was so upset that I called Rae. I hadn't been talking to her much. Her mom hadn't been feeling well, so she was spending all of her time with her. The last thing she needed was to hear about me and the same thing I had been talking about for weeks. I finally got a chance to talk to her, and I will never forget that conversation. I needed her to calm me down. I wanted to tell her what the doctor had said. I let her know that once again they said it was nothing. Rae went on to explain that her mom had a few lumps in the past and they really were nothing. She wasn't trying to dismiss my concern, but she said really it was probably true. Rae went on to say that she was worried about me and she had never seen me this way. I think to be honest that when I couldn't let it go, she either thought I was really losing it or something really was wrong. I could hear worry in her voice. I think she wanted to think I was being OCD but knew by the way I was acting that something was wrong. I told her I didn't know what I was going to do but that I had to do something and it had to be quickly. The fear kept growing and growing. I felt really bad because she had so much on her with her mom and then me as well. I told her I was going to think of something and wasn't sure what it was, but I had to beat the system somehow. I had waited so long that now it was crucial for my life. I let her go and told her I would let her know what I decided to do.

    I didn't sleep at all that night. I lay awake thinking and trying to decide what to do. It was really sad because to be honest I didn't even feel like I could talk it over with Andrew. I didn't want to burden him with all he had going on. I kept it all in trying to figure out what I was going to do. The truth is I was really going through this by myself. I got up the next morning and decided I was going to go to my old hotel and see Katherine. I knew if I went to her, she would help me. I needed a plan, and I needed it yesterday. I got a coffee and headed her way. I called my mom on the way and let her know I was going to see Katherine and maybe she could help. As soon I walked in, I saw her, and she gave me the biggest hug. I knew I was safe and I was with someone that really cared about what I was going through. I looked at her, and my tears started to flow. Katherine let me hug her and get it out. She knew more than anyone how scared I was. It took me a while to get myself together. Once I did, we sat down in the lobby like we used to, and I looked at her and told her how much I needed her help. I told her I truly believed it was a matter of life and death. I told her I believed more than anything that God gave her to me for a reason. I was very worried at that moment as to the real reason he led me to her. I couldn't figure out why everything up to this point had happened. It was hard for me to wrap my head around how I ended up in Indianapolis sitting there feeling like I was fighting for my life. All I did was pray God would carry me through and use the people he had put in my life. I looked at Katherine and told her I needed to find a way to get a mammogram. I let her know I felt for some reason that time was of the essence. I begged her to help me and help me now. She for the first time could tell I was very serious and she had to make it happen. It was no longer something I was a little concerned about. And she realized the spot I had asked her to feel a few weeks earlier was still there and I was not able to let it go. Just as I thought, as soon as we were done and she knew it all, she was on the phone. Katherine had been going to the same doctors and hospitals since she arrived from the Dominican Republic. She trusted all of her people, and I trusted her. I sat there while she made the call and told her friend that was a nurse what was going on. Katherine told her how I needed a mammogram and I needed it now. The nurse told her I could come in the next morning at eight o'clock and to bring my insurance card and my script for it and not to be late. When Katherine got off the phone, I was devastated because I needed a script from my doctor once again. I was so over it. I sat down and cried, feeling so beat down and defeated. A feeling I am not really used to.

Katherine sat down and said it would be all right. She said, "We just have to pray for the answer to come." We sat there and prayed together.

After sitting there for a few minutes, I told her I was going to have to go against everything I stood for. I am not one for lying. I don't like it, and I just think it ends up being more work than it's worth. If you tell one, you can be assured that you will have to follow it up with several more. But I just couldn't live this way. An idea had come to me, and I had decided I was going to do it. It was my only way to get it done once and for all. I was going to call Dr. Smith's office and talk to his head nurse. She was amazing and was always so very helpful. It was my only shot to get my mammogram done at eight o'clock the next morning. I told Katherine I was going to make this happen and I was calling my girl at Dr. Smith's office.

I called her, told her it was me, and started to cry. I was crying so hard. I could barely get my words out. She settled me down enough that I could tell her what I wanted her to do. I told her I truly thought it had reached the point of it being a matter of life and death. I really believed that, and she could finally hear it in my voice. She could tell that I was desperate and I wasn't going to let it go. I reminded her how long I had been worried about this and it was only getting worse. I explained to her I knew what I was asking her could make her lose her job. I let her know if I didn't have this godly feeling about the whole thing I wouldn't be asking her. I let her know she truly was the only one that could make this happen and I would be forever grateful. I couldn't believe my ears, but she said she was going to do it. I started to cry and told her how thankful I was and that she wouldn't be sorry. I promised her that no matter what happened it would never come back on her. I let her know what a great thing she was doing and that she was an angel on earth. So between her and Katherine, I was finally going to the other hospital to have it done. I couldn't believe it. I gave her all the info to the other hospital, and she said she would take care of it. She told me to go as scheduled. I thanked her and let her know she was a godsend. I got off the phone and started crying to Katherine. I told her thank you and that between the two of them I was finally going to get some answers. I said I loved her and left to go get the kids from school.

CHAPTER THIRTY FOUR

I started thinking how I was finally going to find out what was inside of me. I was so relieved and so unsure of everything. The unknown was the scariest part at that moment, but after tomorrow it might be the known that turned out to be the scariest. But no matter what, the feeling I had deep in my gut couldn't be ignored anymore, and no matter the outcome, I had to face it. I called my mom and told her what had happened and that I would be seen tomorrow morning. I started crying because I really wanted her by my side more than anything. I knew it wasn't possible and I would have to do it alone. Rae's mom was ill, and I knew she couldn't come. This would be a time that I had to go at it alone. I can remember the first time I had a mammogram it was with her, and it pained me to do this one alone. It had to be done. There were so many reasons to follow through and get it done and only one reason not to go. The one reason was the same reason as to why I was in this position I was in at this very moment. It was fear and fear alone.

I didn't sleep a wink that night. It was the middle of winter, and the weather was terrible. Andrew was going to have to stay at home with McGraw during my appointment. Remember that Andrew was always working and I was the caretaker of our children. Andrew would also have to drop McKynna off at school. All of it was so hard to handle. I knew that the moment I walked out of our hotel room my entire world could change. I didn't have a good feeling about the outcome. I knew deep in my soul that something was really wrong and this would be the day to bring it to reality instead of leaving it as a nightmare in my head. I had an early appointment. It was at eight o'clock in the morning, and I had never been to this hospital. I remembered sitting by my babies on the bed and not being able to stop looking them. I leaned over to smell their soft hair, gently kissed them both, and asked God to please no matter what allow me to raise my babies. I started to cry and knew I had to let them go; it was time to leave.

The drive to the hospital felt like the longest drive in the world. I actually felt like I was traveling from one end of the world to the other. It was so cold and icy that morning. I called my mom and talked to her the entire time. I can remember her being the loving and optimistic person she has always been. I know I am who I am because of her. I know in my heart that God chose her to be my mom because he knew what I would face in my life and that I would need someone like her to teach me to survive. My mom was my cheerleader and had been my entire life. I knew she wasn't about to fail me now. I could feel how much she wanted to be there. I told her that I was strong and I was going to do this. I talked to her all the way there. It was like I was so scared to hang up the phone. I arrived at the hospital and told her I would call her when it was done. I told her I loved her with every fiber of my being and to just pray. I told her I would feel her love with me. I could tell she was trying to be strong and heard the crack in her voice. She told me she loved me and it was all going to be fine. I tried to call

Rae on the way in but couldn't get her. I knew she probably had a long night with her mom, so I just left her a message. I told her I was going in and I loved her.

I walked in, went up to the receptionist, and told her I was there for an eight o'clock appointment. I gave her my insurance card and information. I could barely fill out my paperwork. My entire body was shaking, and I thought to myself that I had no one's hand to hold. I finally got it done and sat back down. At that very moment, I had this feeling come over me. I can't explain it. I knew something was wrong. So I did what I had been doing for months. I talked to God and asked him for the strength to get me through it. I told him I was so very sorry I thought I didn't have a hand to hold when I had the most important hand to hold. Truly the only hand I should want. I had a terrible feeling and asked the Lord to please hold my hand and not to leave me. I told him I couldn't do it alone and that if I had ever needed him, it was right at this very moment. I was about to go into a full-blown panic attack; it wasn't until that very second when they called my name that I all of a sudden got it together. I took the deepest breath I have ever taken and got up and said I was Christi. They greeted me, took me in, and collected a bit of information, and I had to keep reminding myself this was my first mammogram. I was lying to everyone in that office, and to be honest I felt perfectly fine with that. The only one I wanted to protect was Dr. Smith's nurse. So I had to be very careful with my information. She was really going all out for me, and I couldn't live with myself if she got in trouble. So I played my role very well and acted like I had never had one and that I didn't know what I needed to do. The tech let me know it was all right and she would guide me. She then asked me if I had any concerns or if I was having trouble with anything. I explained to her about what I found and where it was located. She then asked me to go get changed and made a notation on my chart as to where she needed to concentrate.

I got in my dressing room, sat down on the bench in there, and literally was about to throw up. I put my head down and said, "Please, God, don't leave me now." I had never felt so helpless in my life. God was the only thing I could count on at that very moment. Somehow, I felt guilty because I was begging him to help me and I should have been talking to him a lot more before this. I asked him to forgive my complacent actions. I started to cry and didn't think I could do it. This was it—the moment I had needed for a long time—and I didn't think I could do it. The tech came and asked if I was all right, and I told her I needed a few more minutes. I finally got changed, got on my knees, and told God that at that very second I was turning it over to him. I gave it to him.

I went in the room, she got me prepped, and we got started. I was crying the entire time. The tech wasn't the best; she didn't really have a compassionate bone in her body. Not really what I needed at the moment. I told her where I needed her to check for my small lump. I told her I had already been to a few doctors and they told me it was nothing. The time had come for her to check it, and I could tell her entire demeanor had changed. My heart sank, and I knew it was something. She started talking to me in a very weird way. All of a sudden, she became so nice, and I could tell something was really wrong. It was worse than I thought. She started saying things like, "We all don't need all of our body parts, as long as we have good support systems." I couldn't believe my ears. I was dying inside, and I knew at that moment I was in trouble. I mean the kind of trouble we all never think is going to happen to us. It was over, and she asked me to wait for a few moments before I got dressed. She left the room, and I sat in that cold room alone, praying like I had never prayed before. I told God not to leave me no matter what happened from this point. I couldn't keep from crying. All I could think about were my babies and what would happen to them if something happened to me. I couldn't leave my children. I wasn't going to abandon them.

I waited in that room for what felt like a lifetime. The tech finally came back and told me to get dressed. She let me know that she was going to take me back to this waiting room in the office and the radiologist was going to come and talk to me. She then asked if I had anyone with me, and I thought I was going to throw up right there. I told her I was alone. I got dressed, and they escorted me into the room. I immediately called Mom. I couldn't even talk I was crying so hard. I told her that something was really wrong and that they brought me to a room all alone. I told her I was waiting on the radiologist to come in. I was having a panic attack and couldn't even breathe much less tell her what was going on. I can't even imagine now that I am a mother how she must have felt. Her baby girl was far away and was about to hear the worst news she could possibly hear, and she was not there to hold my hand. I could tell her heart was breaking and she was trying to be strong for me. I felt like I waited an eternity. I wouldn't let her off the phone. I was shaking and felt like I was living someone else's life. My mom and I prayed so hard on the phone. We prayed like we never had. My mom let me know we could do this and that it was all going to be all right. I held on to her every word and wanted to believe it so very badly. I tried to have the faith, but I couldn't help but think my life as I knew it was over.

The radiologist finally came in and escorted me to this room that looked like a hospital room. I was terrified beyond measure. They had me lie down and started to go over my films with me. I was trying to listen, but all I could think about was that I had cancer. And that could only mean one thing: I was going to die. I tried to listen to him and all that he was saying, but I couldn't focus. I finally heard him tell me I had two things very wrong: I had a tumor, and I had these things called calcifications in the tumor. He told me that he didn't know the severity of either and needed to have a biopsy. I asked what that was, and he explained it was the only way to determine if it was cancer and exactly what kind and the stage.

I was so overwhelmed. I couldn't believe my ears. Even though I thought it for so very long, I couldn't believe it was actually happening. I looked at him and said I wanted it done right away. He told me to get dressed and meet him outside at the reception desk. I saw him take all my films with him and leave the room.

I started crying and couldn't even get dressed. I was so scared and started praying and telling God how much I trusted and believed in him. I really did, and this wasn't the time to waver. I had to believe that he was going to make it all right. I had all these thoughts in my head that I couldn't make sense of. My thoughts were crazy, and I thought I was going crazy. All I could think about was dying and my kids growing up without their mommy. I walked out and told the girl who I was and that I needed an appointment for a biopsy.

She looked at me and said, "Yes, I have your films, and I have an appointment in two weeks."

I looked at her stunned, and said, "Excuse me! Did you say two weeks? I am sorry, but that won't work for me. I need something a lot sooner. I can't wait two weeks to find out if I have cancer."

She looked at me with this very matter-of-fact look and said, "That is all I have."

I lost it with her. I looked at her and said, "I understand it is not your responsibility, but if it was you or your mother, would you want to wait two weeks to see if it was cancer? I know you wouldn't, " I was so scared and so angry. I was not waiting two weeks, no matter what.

I remember calling Mom and telling her that I was about to lose it with them and that I couldn't wait that long. I told her they were checking and it was taking forever. I was shaking so bad. You know when your nerves are so shaken and you feel cold and clammy all over? I was shivering and couldn't focus on anything other than getting out of there. I was so disoriented that I couldn't find my car. It was freezing outside, and the roads were so icy. A winter storm had come in, and I was not only feeling cold from my nerves but also because the temperature was freezing. I was so scared, and it was literally like I was having an out-of-body experience. It was truly like a nightmare, a full-blown nightmare, except I was awake. A security guard came up to me and asked if I needed help. I was crying and told him yes. I told him I couldn't find my car. He took me on his little cart and drove me around until I found it. I was crying so hard as I got up to go to my car, and I looked at him and said, "God sent you to help me." I thanked him.

He looked at me and said, "It is all going to be all right."

For the first time in my life, I heard those words for what they really meant. I told myself for the first time in my life that I really didn't know that to be true. It was like I heard those words for the very first time. I got in my car and sat there and cried. All of these thoughts were running through my head, and I couldn't make sense of any of them. I didn't even know what to do first. I called my mom and talked to her. I needed her to think for me. I was numb and didn't even know my name. I told her I needed to have the biopsy done and done right away. I told her I knew it. I just knew it. She told me to believe and know that it was all right. We weren't thinking the worst until we knew for certain. I told her I needed to call my sweet angel at Dr. Smith's office. I told my mom she would know what to do. I hung up with Mom and called the nurse immediately. I was crying so hard she didn't even know who I was at first. She told me to calm down and start from the beginning. I explained to her what all had just taken place. I let out this huge burst of tears and told her I had known something was terribly wrong all along. I let her know they wanted to wait two weeks for me to have the biopsy done. I said there was no way I could wait that long. I told her that I needed it done now. The feeling I had was real, and I knew there was something really bad happening inside of me. I told her I knew deep in my soul that if I waited, it could mean my life. Once again she could hear it in my voice. She asked if I was driving, and I said yes. She asked me to pull over and not to drive while we talked. I was so scared, and I listened to her. I pulled over on the side of the road. I waited on hold for her for several minutes. It felt like an eternity. I waited with every beat of my heart. It was so weird. I had never heard my heart beat so loud in my life. All I wanted was to have it keep beating. I had a baby at home and one in school, and all I wanted was to see them grow.

The nurse finally came on and said, "I told Dr. Smith the entire story, and he is taking care of you."

I told her I had a long drive back to my hotel in the bad weather. She told me to drive and listen for my phone. Dr. Smith was making arrangements, and he wanted me back at his hospital today. I told her thank you from the bottom of my heart. I let her know she was my angel and that without her none of this would be happening.

I started driving, and I could barely keep my foot on the pedal. I called my mom first and let her know they were working it out. I can't even imagine how she must have felt. Her baby girl was in the worst position she could ever be in, and she was thousands of miles away. I told her I had to call Rae and I would call her when I got back to the hotel. She said all right and that she was praying endlessly. I called Rae right away and told her they had found something. I let her know about the tumor and the calcifications and how they were two separate problems. There was a long pause on the phone, and I asked her if she was still there.

She said, "Yes, I am here." She couldn't believe her ears. She finally said, "You knew it the entire time. You kept telling me, and I didn't really think it would be anything."

I could tell she was not only worried about me but also just wasn't herself. I asked her if she was all right, and she said that her mom was really bad and she didn't know how much longer she would last. This was one of the worst days of my life. We were like sisters and both going through the worst times in our lives without each other. I told her I was sorry and I loved her with all my heart. I told her I would be there in spirit like always. I told her I was right there with her. All of a sudden, I looked up, and Dr. Smith's office was calling. I told her I would call her back.

I clicked over, and the nurse was on the other line. She let me know that Dr. Smith had already set up my appointment with the only breast doctor he used. She said, "He only trusts her."

I said, "I trust him so I trust her."

She let me know that my appointment was at one o'clock. I told her I would be there. She gave me all my instructions.

I got back to the hotel where my baby boy and Andrew were. I let Andrew know what they found and that it wasn't looking so great. He looked at me and said it was just a test and they would confirm it was nothing. All I wanted was to hug my baby. I can remember taking McGraw and holding him like never before. I looked at his little hands and feet. They were the most beautiful hands and feet I had ever laid my eyes on. I wanted to hold on to the feeling I felt when I was holding him. I thought if I could think of this feeling during my test, then I could do it. Once again I had to go at it alone. Andrew would keep McGraw, and I told him I would hopefully be out in time to pick up McKynna. I wanted to see her beautiful face. So before I knew it, I was on my way to my appointment.

The sun had come out, so it would be a better drive. It was very cold outside, but the sun was helping. Oh, how I needed my mom. I wanted her there so badly to help me go through with it. Do you even understand how badly I wanted to turn around? But I had an even bigger fear of not going. I had this long talk with God on the way. I literally talked to him out loud in the car as if he were sitting right next to me. To be honest that was how I liked talking to him the most. I had done it as a little girl. I used to think if I talked to him out loud, he could hear me above the rest. I thought for some odd reason he would just stop what he was doing and take care of me. And, right now, I needed to believe that theory. It was like that was my best bet before entering that building. My sure bet was God. My only bet was God. So I told him in the car to please hold my hand and not let go. I told him to please help me and give me his strength. I told him my life was in his hands and I was going to handle whatever was going to be handed to me.

CHAPTER THIRTY FIVE

I arrived at the hospital and had no idea where to go. I got out of the car and went in the main entrance. I asked the volunteer where exactly her office was, and she directed me. Once again I went in and let them know I was there. I filled out all my paperwork, and all I could do then was wait. I waited for what seemed like forever, but they finally called my name. The sweetest nurse opened the door and called my name. I will never forget what I had on. It was right before Valentine's Day weekend, so I had on a beautiful red sweater. I was trying so hard to be positive. I can remember she smiled so sweetly at me and led me to a room. Julie, introduced herself, and little did I know what a vital role she would play in my life and that she would become a lifelong friend. I was sitting on the table, and she was asking me all kinds of questions. I started to cry and told her how sorry I was. I told her I was trying to be strong but it was so hard. I explained to her what had happened and gave her my films. I gave her all the information she asked for and then some. I barely made it through. I was so emotional, and for some reason she was very easy to talk to. I asked her so many questions, and she didn't care. I know why God puts people in their positions. God puts us where we need to be at the perfect time. I will never forget her and how she made me feel. Julie, told me all about Dr. Wynn and how wonderful she was. When it was time for the doctor to come in, believe it or not, I was actually ready to talk to her. God heard my prayer, and it was weird because it was like he made me calm so I could really listen to her. God knew I was alone in that room and I was the only one that would be listening to her and finding out my future. My heart was heavy, and to be honest I couldn't believe I was in there all by myself. I looked up and told God I was sorry. I knew I wasn't alone and the one thing I had with me was the most important: Him.

So she walked in the room, and I loved her from the moment I met her. She was beautiful and confident. I knew I was in the right hands and if anyone could help me, it was her. I trusted her from the moment I met her. She had a great bedside manner and a grace about her. What she wanted to know first was me. She wanted to get to know me as an individual. I couldn't believe it. I told her about my family and how much I loved my children. I explained to her my long ordeal just to be sitting in the room with her. I still didn't let on that I had other mammograms and that this wasn't my first go-around with all of this. I let her believe this was my only one. I didn't want anyone to get into trouble. I was exactly where I was supposed to be. I started to tell her why I wanted to get the mammogram and that two different doctors had told me it was nothing. I explained to her I couldn't let it go and I had to be sure. I told her how I had lain awake so many nights worried about cancer. For some reason I just couldn't stop thinking about it and that I had it. I told her to please help me. I begged her to prove to me that it wasn't. She told me how the biopsy was going to be taken. The sample would have to be sent off, and then we would have to wait on the results. The bad thing was it was a Friday and I would have to wait over the weekend. It was going to be brutal waiting.

She said she would rush it. The entire thing was very scary, and I was so intimidated. After the test I got dressed, and she said I was going to go back downstairs to have another mammogram done. I still don't understand all of it to this day. I was so sore from the biopsy and wasn't really up for another test. Nonetheless, I had to go and have it done. I think it was to make sure they got a lot of it.

I got dressed, and Dr. Wynn came back in and talked to me a little bit before I went downstairs for the mammogram. She had the sample in her hand, and I asked if I could see it. I looked at it, and it looked so weird. To think that is what they send off to see if I am going to die or not. I looked at her and thanked her for everything. I told her that she made a horrible situation doable. I started to cry and asked her to tell me one thing. I told her I knew I couldn't hold her to it but asked, if she had to say one way or the other, if she thought it was or was not. I wanted to know with every ounce of my being what her opinion was. I sat on the table holding my breath and looking into her eyes. I grabbed her hand and said, "Please! Give me something to go on. It is Valentine's Day weekend, and I need to know what you are thinking, good or bad."

She let out a really big sigh and said, "All right. I will tell you what I think about the sample, but it's only my opinion. It holds no truth. Do you understand?"

I told her yes.

At that moment she held up the sample and showed it to me. She asked if I saw how it moved in the jar. She gave me examples and educated me on how she was coming up with her opinion. She looked at me and said, "If I had to take a guess right now on what I see, I would say it is *not cancer.*"

I bent my head down and started to cry like I had never cried before. I somehow had hoped I would feel better if she said she thought it was all right, but once again I didn't feel at ease in any sense.

She put her hand on me and said, "It is going to be fine."

I looked up with a look of desperation and said, "Is it something I did? Is it because I drink Diet Coke and coffee?" I asked if I was going to die because I didn't take care of my body. I cried in my hands and felt more helpless than I ever had in my life. I told her I had two babies and couldn't leave them. They needed me, and I couldn't leave them now. I looked at her and asked her what was going to happen to me. I told her to please save me. I will never forget the words she said to me.

She said, "If it is cancer, your life will change for just a little while, and then you will be as good as new."

I looked at her and said, "Please help me."

She said, "I will."

At that very moment, looking at her, I had to put all my trust in her and believe I was sitting in her room for a reason. Like I said, people enter our lives for a reason, and I knew God put me there for a purpose. I had to know it was to live. I put my head in my hands and asked her to save me. I let her know if it was in fact cancer, I would be the best patient she had ever had. I would do whatever she said to do in order to live. I had to live for my children. And something so weird I felt right at that very moment was that somehow they would push me and get me through. Dr. Wynn looked at me and told me she was sending me downstairs for one more mammogram to make sure they got what they needed for the biopsy.

I looked at her and said with a shaken voice, "I hope this isn't the beginning of the end."

Dr. Wynn looked at me and said, "It is all going to be all right, and I want you to go have a great Valentine's Day weekend with your family."

As soon as Julie came back into the room, she looked at me, and I burst into tears. I looked at her and said, "I'm so scared, Julie."

When she looked at me with her sweet and kind face, I could tell she was struggling. I know she was struggling for the words to help me. She saw the desperation in my face and desperately wanted to say what I wanted to hear. Julie said, "I want you to know one thing. No matter what we aren't going to leave your side, and you couldn't be in a better place."

Believe it or not, it was what I needed to hear. I was so scared and really thought I was going to die. In the blink of an eye, I started thinking about whom I wanted with me and how much. The most important people and the people I wanted with me at that moment were nowhere near. I told Julie I could feel that she meant what she was saying and it meant the world to me. She literally helped me get dressed and then get downstairs. I didn't think I was going to be able to walk down there. Julie set it all up and walked with me. When she passed me off, I was dying inside. I had gotten comfortable with her and desperately wanted her to stay. However, I was one of millions who had just found out they may have cancer. I hugged her and thanked her, and she let me know I was going to be in good hands.

They took me back, put me in another room, and told me to get changed. I will never forget it. The sweet girl who took me back was so young and had a beautiful smile. It somehow gave me comfort. I looked at her and said, "In here?"

She said, "Yes, and everything you need is in there."

I started crying as she left me in the room alone. Once again I found myself in a room getting changed for another test. I had to sit down and talk to God. I mean really talk to him. Praying is what we all do. Praying is vital to keeping our faith where it needs to be on a continuous basis. Having said that, in moments such as this one, a full-blown conversation is what it takes. I sat down and started talking to him and begging him for the strength I needed to get through this one last test. I was completely exhausted and didn't think I had it in me to do one more test, much less receive more bad news. I couldn't do it without the help of God. So I sat down, looked up, and said, "I am begging you to hold me in the palm of your hands and get me through this. No matter what comes, hold on to me." I told him I was turning it over to him and to please make me strong. I knew he was aware of my weaknesses and that he was my only hope. There wasn't one person or thing that could get me through, only him.

The tech came and knocked on the door, and I told her I was ready. When she opened the door, I started to cry and told her how scared I was. I will never forget how she took my hand and said, "I'll be here with you the entire time." She asked me a few questions and needed to get more information from me. She looked at me and said, "Are you all right?"

I let her know I really wasn't and that it had been an extremely long day. After she looked at my chart, I explained this was it for me. They had found something bad, and they are still testing. She asked if she could give me a hug, and I said sure. God knew just what I needed. A hug was exactly what I needed. I hugged her and cried more. I told her thank you and that it really meant a lot.

They got the test done, and I bled all over the place. The biopsy made it hard to do the second mammogram. They had to clean me up and everything around me. It was very painful. It was a nightmare, and I didn't even know if I had cancer or not. I got it together and went back and tried to get dressed. It wouldn't stop bleeding so I had to call them in. I called my mom and told her what was going on. I had never broken a bone, and here I was dealing with all this. They brought supplies, cleaned me up again, and bandaged it all up. It was time to put on a brave face and go to my babies. They had done all they needed to determine if I indeed had cancer. Now over the Valentine's Day weekend all we could do was wait. I checked out and asked them the earliest they would contact me. I told them I was so scared and to please rush it if they could. They let me know Dr. Wynn had a rush on them. I thanked them for everything and left.

CHAPTER THIRTY SIX

As I was walking out, everything suddenly looked so different. I had the weirdest feeling I have ever had. I called Andrew and told him I was on my way. On the way home, I called my mom and told her I needed her now. She said she and my dad where packing and to book her on the next flight out. I did exactly that. Before I knew it, I was picking up my parents at the airport and trying to get through the longest weekend in my life. My parents were very supportive, and I don't know how I would have made it through that weekend without the two of them. I had come home and told Andrew everything, but I think he was still very much in denial. I know he thought it was going to be nothing. In his heart he knew my tests were going to be negative, when I knew deep in my soul that all this worrying and anxiety I had for months was for a reason. And the reason was that I had breast cancer. I had never felt so strongly about anything in my life. I hoped I would be wrong but somehow knew I wouldn't.

The weekend went by very slowly, and to this day that Valentine's Day is a complete blur. I went through the motions and prayed continuously. I thought we were going to get the results on Monday. I didn't sleep a wink that Sunday night. I didn't want to shut my eyes because I knew I would be waking up to the day my life would change forever. My mom was pretty much up with me all night. I know she knew that deep in my heart I knew I had it. It was killing her. We went down and had coffee. We had moved to the other hotel and had only been there a few days. They were very kind, and the hotel was comfortable.

I asked Andrew when he came down and was leaving for work if he would call them and see if they had my results. I will say he was always good about following through with things I couldn't. We were all in the lobby and waited anxiously while he called. He walked away from me and made the call. I had never felt so vulnerable in my life. I think I held my breath until I almost passed out. I was sitting at a table with my parents and the kids when he walked up.

He looked at me and said, "They won't have them until later on today. It is still too early."

I leaned down, put my head on the table, and cried. I was so tired and just didn't want to wonder anymore. My parents held me and told me it was all in God's perfect timing. I couldn't have been happier they were there. Andrew left for work, and I got the kids together for school. I pulled it together and made it like any other morning. I knew I was in for a long day again. There is nothing harder than waiting on someone to call you and tell you if you are dying.

I spent the day with my parents. After lunch we went back to the hotel, and I met Andrew there. I asked him to call them for the results before I went and got the kids. Once again we were all in the lobby. I had my cell phone, and Andrew had his. He told me he had a business call he was waiting on and to call from my phone. I got the number and could barely dial it. Andrew took the phone and made the call. We were on hold for the doctor when he got his call. My stomach sank when I heard Dr. Wynn come on the line. She said, "Is this Christi?"

I said, "Yes, it is me." I asked her if she had the results.

There was silence on the phone, and she said, "Yes, I do." I was trying so hard to focus on what she was saying. She started talking about the sample of the biopsy. All I wanted to know was if I had cancer or not.

I finally stopped her and said, "I don't understand anything you are saying." I asked her very loud and bluntly, "Do I have *cancer*?" My heart was pounding, and I couldn't breathe. I had the biggest lump in my throat.

My parents were standing at the end of the hallway looking at me, and Andrew was right in front of me. Andrew was mouthing to me and saying, "It's not right." He kept asking me over and over.

And I will never forget her words: "Yes, Christi, it is cancer."

I said, "I am sorry. What did you say?"

She replied, "Yes, I am sorry to say it is cancer."

I looked at Andrew and said, "I told you. I knew it was cancer." I handed him the phone and walked over to the wall to keep myself from falling. Everything I had been scared of since I could remember had just become reality. I had breast cancer. My parents came to me, and we all cried. I knew I was going to die and was not going be able to raise my beautiful children. How was I going to tell them they weren't going to have their mommy? All I could think about was how long I had to teach them everything I wanted to teach them. I was going to have to teach them a lifetime of lessons in God only knew how short of a time. I was devastated and was really praying that my instincts where wrong. But they weren't; they were very real.

Andrew, I think, was more surprised than any of us. He had made himself believe it wasn't true and that it was a false alarm. I can only imagine what he was thinking at that moment. He didn't say much; however, he went into his quiet mode. I had handed off the phone to him, and he got the information on our next step. He said that we wouldn't know any more until we met with Dr. Wynn. Andrew said they needed a few more days so we wouldn't go see them until Wednesday. I had so many emotions running through my body, and to tell you the truth, I thought I was in a dream. I was so angry that I had to wait again. I walked over to the couch in the lobby and sat down and cried. I cried for so many reasons. Mostly I cried because of fear. I was so scared for my children and me. It was the unknown that was in front of me. I had no idea what I was about to face. At that very moment, I didn't think I knew what the word *brave* meant. I had my family and my children to see me through. Again, it was the longest two days.

    I decided not to say anything to the kids until I had my first appointment and knew more. I had to really think about what all I was going to tell them and how I would actually be able to explain to them that mommy was sick. The hardest part was I didn't even feel sick or look sick. So trying to explain any of this to them was going to be as tough as moving mountains. I couldn't even wrap my head around it, much less ask them to try to understand any of it.

    I not only had to tell them but call my best friend in the whole world and tell her I had cancer. Everything with her mom, and now I had to tell her my fears were warranted. I had it, and I needed her desperately. I needed to be there for her at this time in her life, and now I was sick. I knew I needed to make the call, so I did. I called her, and when she answered, I could tell her voice was tired. I could tell she didn't want to talk, but she answered anyway. I told her I knew she was so tired and I wouldn't keep her long, but I had gotten my results back. Before I could tell her, she started crying. Now let me say Rae isn't one to cry or show emotion. It takes a lot for her to cry. I asked her if she was all right, and she replied, "No, I'm not." She told me how much she loved me and wished I was with her because her mom had just passed away. I stood there holding my phone in complete disbelief. I couldn't get one word out. All I could think about was that her mother just died and her best friend was calling her to tell her she had been diagnosed with breast cancer. I was asking myself how much one person could take on a single day. I started to cry, and I told her I loved her and how sorry I was I wasn't able to be by her side. She stopped for a minute and said, "Wait, what were the results? Everything is good, right?" I was very silent for what seemed like an eternity. She said, "Christi!"

I started crying, and I said, "I am so sorry, Rae. It is cancer. I have breast cancer."

I could tell that she couldn't take it. She sat down on the cold bathroom floor and cried. I told her I knew she was dealing with so much with her mom and I wouldn't have any information for a few more days. I told her I would call her after my appointment and fill her in. It was so much to handle for us both. We both wanted to be there for each other desperately, but it would have to be from the heart. I told her we were going to be together through prayer and God would keep us together over the miles.

CHAPTER THIRTY SEVEN

The morning of my appointment finally arrived, and I could barely get dressed. I found myself staring at myself in the mirror. I couldn't get past looking at who I was at the moment and knowing what I was going to become. I knew I had to get it together and quick. In addition to all that, my back was still really hurting me. I didn't say anything to anyone, especially now. I was very scared that the cancer had moved all over and was in my back. I knew if I said something, they would do more tests. Part of me didn't want to know how bad it really was and to just live as long as I could without any help. I was so scared of what was running around in my body.

In the meantime my sister, Caryn, made it in. I was glad to have my family around me to give me strength. I needed them more than I can say. We all got there and were seated in a big boardroom. There was a huge table and lots of chairs. The room looked as serious as my condition. The room started to fill up with people. I wasn't ready for any of this, but it didn't seem to matter. I was about to enter a life that I never thought possible, and I had to pull it together if I wanted to survive. We sat down at the big table while we were waiting for everyone to enter the room. Andrew sat down next to me, and I reminded him that I was not going to mention my back. I warned him to not bring it up. He said I had to tell them, and I insisted we not bring it up right at this moment. I told him to give me time and I would let Dr. Wynn know when I was ready.

There was a great lady that entered the room first. She was a volunteer, and she let me know she would be my go-to person from here on. She let me know that I could count on her for anything. I couldn't believe how sweet and caring she was. She let us know she was a survivor herself and now she volunteered to help others. She brought lots of information and a folder to keep everything organized. It looked so large and full of lots of information. I was so in over my head I didn't hear most of what she said. I asked her if she knew anything about my results. Sadly she knew nothing. She said the doctor would be in in a few minutes.

Then I looked up, and my sweet Julie entered the room and gave me the biggest hug. If she only knew how much I needed it. I could tell she would be a vital part of my journey from the beginning. She was the one along with Dr. Wynn that told me on that awful day it was all going to be all right. Oddly enough the words stuck, and I had no other choice than to believe them. God sent me to that office with them for a reason. They were my cancer family from the moment we said hello.

I started to calm down somewhat and tried to think positive. My mom sat on the other side of me, and my sister got a chair and sat in the corner. I could tell she was very scared and uncomfortable. I know it was so hard on her, and I was very grateful she was there. We hadn't been together for a while and I was so very glad she was there. Looking at my mom and my sister, I felt very blessed and loved.

Dr. Wynn walked in, and all I could think was, this is it, God, game on. They were all talking, and I was sitting in that room having the most important talk with God I had ever had. This was it, and I would find out my fate. They would tell me right then and there what it was going to take to live. So I told God to hold my hand. Here we go.

I finally tuned in to what they were saying and tried to listen to every word. Dr. Wynn pulled out this folder, and she sat across the table from me and Andrew. There were a lot of words and numbers on the paper. She started to explain them in her words. I finally looked at her and said, "I am just not getting any of this." I started to cry and get overwhelmed again, a feeling I would get used to for months to come. It was a feeling I would have to learn to control along with so many others. My tears were pouring out, and my heart was breaking. I had cancer, and I was finding out if I could even fight for my life. She finally started talking in my words. I had a very aggressive cancer called triple negative. It meant that my cancer was not related to hormones. I had a ductal carcinoma, which a lot of women have, but mine was one of the most aggressive. It would travel faster than if it were hormonal related. They have more options when it isn't triple negative. But of course I felt like it was par for the course for her to tell me the bad news. I was only a stage one, and that was a blessing. However, the fact that it was so aggressive was a game changer for my case. I was only forty-one, and that meant I had a lot of years for it to return. That was a big factor.

Dr. Wynn explained it all, looked at me, and said, "We have a lot of decisions to make, Christi. We need to decide and get everything scheduled."

Andrew and I have always looked at things differently. And that is all right. We all have our own opinions, but that is all they are. Ultimately we all have to make our own decisions and do what is best for ourselves. We are the ones that have to live with our choices. Let me say this applies to everything in life. Not just medically. When I spoke earlier in my book about how we all have our cancers, whether they are physical or some other mountain we are climbing, we have to make our own choices. Hoping that we allow God to help us make those choices. Dr. Wynn said that I had two choices. She let me know that because it was caught at stage one, they could perform a lumpectomy and possibly apply a little radiation, and I would be good to go. I would still have to undergo lots of tests for years to come, but we would just have to stay on top of it for the rest of my life. I asked her if that was my only option.

She said, "No, you have the option to have a single or a double mastectomy."

I told her I read up on those procedures, and it was something I really wanted to explore. I felt strongly about the double because it really cut the percentage down on it coming back. I was so young and desperately wanted to live. I was willing to do whatever I had to in order to live. Andrew spoke up right away and said I shouldn't be drastic and we should talk about it.

I looked at him and said, "No disrespect to you, but this will be my decision." I told him I would do what I had to and there was nothing too drastic to save my life. The conversation went back and forth with everyone in the room giving their opinion. I looked at Andrew and said, "I will decide." I asked Dr. Wynn if I could see her in private. She said of course. We walked out, and she took me into another room.

I looked at her and told her I had to do this my way. I had listened to myself up to this point, and I thanked God every second that he gave me that gift. I started to cry and told her I knew what I needed to do for me. I know what is best for me and consequently what is best for my babies. I wanted the cancer out, and I wanted it to stay out. It wasn't welcome anywhere in my temple. I told her my mind was made up. They were both coming off. The funny thing is it was never a question in my mind. It is like God was letting me pave my road and he was giving me the strength to do it. I was so scared and couldn't believe I had to make all of these decisions at such a young age. But I knew I could do it. Dr. Wynn told me that at my age she wasn't surprised I had decided to go through with the double. I told her I wanted it done as soon as I could.

We both returned to the other room, and I told Andrew and the others my decision. The only thing that mattered to me at that moment was making good choices to save myself. I had made my choice and just wanted to see it through. So we were wrapping up and getting things scheduled, and Andrew mentioned my back. I started to cry and told him to please let it go. Dr. Wynn asked if there was anything else we needed to discuss. I told her no and that I was all right. Andrew then told her that I had been having trouble with my lower back. And I put my head down and cried like I have never cried. I was so scared, and if the cancer had spread, I didn't want to know. I said it was nothing and for her not to worry about it.

She said, "I will worry, and I need to know what is going on."

I was crying so hard I had to take a minute to even be able to tell her. I finally got it out that my lower back had been bothering me and sometimes the pain was bad. She asked her nurse to get a copy of my body scan. The nurse looked and couldn't find one.

Dr. Wynn looked at me and said, "Did they ever give you a full-body scan?"

I said "No."

She said, "It will show us if the cancer has spread." She wasn't happy and told one of the nurses she couldn't believe it hadn't already been done. She wanted it done yesterday. They set it up for Friday morning.

As they were doing that, another nurse came in and gave me some information about this genetic testing called the BRCA test. There is a BRCA1 and a BRCA2. I had all of sudden remembered seeing all the posters in Dr. Smith's office. I had even talked about it with my mom before when I had my checkup. I couldn't believe I was going to have another test. And a test I really didn't need. I felt exhausted and was pretty much over all of it already. Dr. Wynn explained to me that only roughly 1 percent of doctors in the country test for it at this time. I really didn't even fall under the qualifications to be tested. This gave me more reason to believe that the Lord has his hand in everything we do. The chance of my going to a doctor that took such preventative measures with her patients was a true miracle in itself. All of the events that had led up to this very moment and this very test were all perfectly orchestrated by God himself. That is all I can say. To this day when you talk about the BRCA gene, a lot of people don't have a clue as to what you are talking about. Remember, I didn't have breast cancer on either side of my family. I was the chosen one. However, as I was so young, she felt very strong about testing me for it. She felt very confident that I would not have it but wanted to just rule it out. In one breath I was thankful for her and in another I was tired and didn't want any more tests for which I could receive bad results. I asked her what it involved, and she simply said it was a blood test. They would send it off to Salt Lake City, UT to be tested. I agreed, and they took my blood in the office and sent it off the next day. That was really all I thought about that because she really just wanted to rule it out. There was really no worry. Besides, I had so many concrete results right in front of me, and I was going to be scanned in the next few days. I was terrified and so angry with Andrew. I knew it was for the better and I needed it done, but I wasn't ready to say anything about my back. I was still trying to process the cancer in my left breast.

CHAPTER THIRTY EIGHT

So as you can already guess, I didn't sleep once again. My mom didn't either. It seemed to be a trend with us. Sleep wasn't in our life at that moment. Besides, I really took the saying "You'll get plenty of sleep when you die" to heart. So here we were again, back to the imaging office to have the scan done. I was so terrified, and I couldn't have anyone go in with me. It was all highly radioactive, so I had to do it alone.

It was so cold that morning. The sun was out, but it was so windy. I had to go to a separate building outside to take the test, and I had to ride on this open lift to get up to the door to enter. They came and got me to take me out to the building. Once we were outside, we had to wait on the lift to come down so I could get on. As it was on its way down, I noticed a girl that was coming down. I watched her as she came down. For the first time, I thought to myself how that could be me. Her hair was gone. I looked at her, and my eyes filled up. As she stepped off the lift, I know she felt me staring at her, and she looked at me and gave me a big smile. You could tell she was tired and worn out, but she found a way to smile at me. I will never forget it. It was like she could feel how scared I was and it was her way of telling me it was going to be all right. I smiled back as she walked past me. From that point on, I always told myself if she could smile, I could too.

I went in and had to drink this terrible drink so they could do the scan. They put you in a room all alone and let you lie in a recliner and drink the liquid until it was gone. As I was lying there, they played country music. I was so grateful because I thought it would get my mind off the test. One of the defining moments in my journey was that day sitting in my recliner waiting to take a test that would show me if my body had been taken over by cancer. It truly was going to tell me what I was in for. So lying there listening to the music, my defining moment came. When the song by Brad Paisley and Dolly Parton came on, I really couldn't believe my ears. I lay there and listened to the words to that song. I was fighting for my life, and hearing that song somehow made me calm down and start to look at things differently. I listened to every word. It gave me peace, and as I listened to it, I realized that no matter what happened it was going to be just how it was meant to be. I knew I wasn't ready to go, but I believe God wanted me to hear that song at that very moment. I took it as a sign and told God I would never give up on surviving. I would do what I had to. However, I think God also wanted me to know that no matter what happened I would be taken care of. No matter the outcome, he would take care of me. I went on to take my test and turned it over to the Lord. At that point that was all I could do. Once again it was given on a Friday, and I wouldn't be able to find out my results until Tuesday. I think the waiting was harder than anything. The parts of my journey when I had to deal with unknowns were truly when my faith was tested. I mean really tested. I had to know he was always sitting right beside me. My faith couldn't waver. In my position it wasn't an option to not have my faith.

Andrew tried to call my counselor on Saturday to see if they had any results, and they had nothing. It would be Tuesday. I was driving on Monday morning and still hadn't heard anything. I was with my mom and my sister when I got a call. It was from one of the nurses at Dr. Wynn's office. I thought they were going to give me the results of my scan. When she got me on the phone, she asked me if I was home, and I told her I was in the car. She then asked me to pull over so we could talk. I said, "What do you need to tell me?" I started crying and pulled over right away. I was so upset and in a panic.

She said, "Christi, it is just another small setback."

I said, "What? What else is going on?"

She said, "I don't know how to tell you this, but you tested positive for the BRCA1 gene."

I had forgotten all about even taking that test, and now they were telling me I had that gene. I thought to myself, you have got to be kidding. I was so sick I didn't think I could even make it home. I was screaming and just couldn't believe it. My mom and my sister had to calm me down and get me together. I was like, are you kidding me? It didn't even run in our family, and I had it. I was at a loss. I really started to wonder what I had done to have all this coming my way. Had I done something so bad to deserve all of this? I know you don't ask questions or question God, but enough was enough. Now I had to focus on a whole new set of problems. I knew nothing about it because honestly I didn't think I would be a carrier. The entire ball game changed. The chances of my cancer coming back went to about 87 percent. Well, I had already gotten breast cancer, and now I had to worry about ovarian cancer. Are you kidding me? The one thing I had so much anxiety about was exactly the gene I HAD. I sat there in disbelief and asked myself, could this be real? I guess it could because I was just told it was. She said that my entire plan would change and I would have to talk to Dr. Wynn.

I was on my way back to the hotel when Andrew called me on my phone. I was crying and asked him if he knew. He told me yes and asked if I would meet him at the hotel. I said I was almost there. I waited for him in the lobby. When he got there, I saw a look on his face that I had never seen. I was going to have a double mastectomy and be done. *No one* had said anything about chemo. As it was stage one, I believed I wasn't going to have to do it. And Andrew came to the hotel to deliver more horrible news. When Dr. Wynn called Andrew, they discussed the facts, and she let him know that having the gene changed my entire defense against both the cancer and the BRCA. I would have to take precautionary chemo.

Now I not only had triple-negative cancer but also a terrible gene that could bring it back and cause it to spread. I was truly about to go out of my mind. I can remember looking up and asking God if he was really serious right now. I was so angry at that very moment. I was speechless. I thought my road at that moment was looking pretty rough. I thought I had it figured out, and then the hits just kept on coming. I couldn't believe I was being told I would have to put that poison in my body. I said from the very beginning I was going to do what it took to make sure it never came back. It was way more than what I thought it would be. I was told I had an oncology appointment set up for me. They wanted me to get started right away. And in the meantime I realized I still hadn't gotten my results from my scan. It felt like it was taking forever.

CHAPTER THIRTY NINE

Tuesday came, and we all got ready and headed out to the cancer center. I was going to meet my oncologist for the first time. It was all one big family. The facility that was taking care of me was truly a dream come true. My entire team of doctors just blew me away time after time. I wasn't a number. I was treated as an individual that they truly were committed to doing everything in their power to save me. I was blessed in more ways than I can even begin to say. When I got to the center, honestly I almost lost it. Looking around I couldn't believe I was going to be a patient there. I thought I was living someone else's life. Reality sets in when you are waiting and then you hear them call your name. It doesn't get more real than that. They called me, and we all went back. They took all my vitals and weighed me before they assigned us a room. They put us in a room, and we waited until my oncologist came in.

I remember thinking how young and pretty she was. I felt comfortable with her. I was very pleased with her. She started asking questions and getting my personal information. I could tell she was very concerned that my cancer was triple negative. I liked her and the way she spoke to me. She started talking about my results and things I knew nothing about.

I said, "I am so sorry. What are you talking about?"

She looked at me and said, "Didn't they call you with the results of your scan?"

I said, "No, they didn't. I haven't heard a thing."

She looked at me and said it was great. "The cancer hasn't traveled to any major organs in your body."

I looked at her and let out this huge scream and started to cry. McGraw was there, and he got so excited for me. I will never forget when he looked at his mommy and said, "Did we win, Mommy? Did we win?"

I looked at my angel and said, "Yes, baby, we won this one. We won this one." We all were so happy, and I hugged him harder than I ever knew I possibly could. I then looked up and said, "Are you sure?"

She looked at me and said, "Yes. We won't know about your lymph nodes or if it is outside of the tumor until your surgery, but as far as your organs go, they are all good."

I felt the biggest relief; you would have thought they said I was cured. I knew I had a long road ahead, but that was the best news I could have gotten right then. We then talked about things that were up in the air until I had my surgery, regarding my nodes and margins. I wasn't sure what it all meant and didn't want to ask any more questions. I was so tired and just wanted that appointment to be over. The reality was I was going to be back there really soon. But there were things I needed to know and wanted to prepare myself for. As badly as I didn't want to ask, I needed answers. I remembered vaguely what my grandmother had gone through with the chemotherapy, and I was sick to my stomach thinking about having to do it. I wasn't prepared for that part of it. I didn't think I was going to need it. Well, I was, and I had to face it. I looked at her and asked her what would happen to me.

She said, "I am not sure what you are asking."

I said, "The side effects of the chemo. Can you tell me what happens to people who take it?"

She said, "Well, the two that you are taking have many side effects. But the two most noticeable are going to be weight gain and hair loss."

I couldn't help but let the tears flow. I looked at her and said, "So I will bald and fat. Is that what you are saying?" All I could think about was losing my hair. I could handle the weight thing, but my hair was another story altogether. How would I tell my children who are just babies that Mommy was not going to have her long dark hair anymore? I thought of McGraw right away. Since I breastfed him, McGraw had held on to my long hair to fall asleep. I couldn't imagine even telling him that all my hair was going to fall out.

The most important thing for me was how my children were going to get through this. I wanted them to come out of this as little scared as possible. It was really all about them. I mean it had to be about me so I could make it about them. I knew the only way for them to have the life I dreamed for them and that they deserved was for this to be about me and for me to survive. I was crying for so many reasons. But, at that very moment, I would be lying if I said I wasn't sitting on that table crying at the thought of losing my beautiful, long, dark hair. I don't mind saying it was one of my best features.

Right at that moment, McGraw walked up to me and said, "Mommy, why are you crying if we won?"

My heart was breaking inside, and I looked at him and said, "They are happy tears, baby. Mommy is happy." I looked at him and realized I had to be strong and let him know every second of every day it was all going to be all right.

He looked at me and said, "Can we go now, Mommy?"

I looked at him and said, "Yes, we can go now, baby. We are done for now."

He said, "I am so proud of you, Mommy."

I gave him the biggest hug and said, "And I am proud of you too, my sweet boy." I told him what a good boy he was.

She said, "You will get your next appointment out front at the desk. You need to remember I won't see you until after your surgery, and we'll find out more once they get in there."

I told her I understood and I would see her soon. We left and went to pick up McKynna. That appointment was so emotionally draining. I was so tired, and all I wanted to do was be with my children and rest. I didn't even know if that was possible. I knew I had a lot to do before my surgery because I would be down for a while. I was getting organized and decided to focus on one thing at a time. One hurdle at a time was all I could handle. My double mastectomy was first, and I had to get my head and heart around it. I was forty-one years old, and my entire body was about to change, starting with a part I was quite fond of. Let's be honest: we all have things we like about ourselves, and I was very blessed with my chest.

That night I went into the bathroom, and I remember running the water for my bath and while waiting looking at myself in the mirror and trying to prepare myself for my new set. I had decided to have reconstruction at the same time as the removal. The surgery time was really pushing it, but I didn't care. I wasn't about to come out of that operating room with nothing. Here is the thing: everyone has his or her own way of looking at things. It is all right for everyone to feel and believe differently. That is the way God made us. But for me in my situation and my emotional state, I had to have it done all at once. It was the way I wanted it. No questions were to be asked about it. I didn't care how long the surgery was or about the recovery time. I wanted to feel as complete after the removal as I possibly could. This was the only way I could do it.

I had a few weeks to get everything settled and prepared before it would be done. I knew that God was right there on the same page with me. I knew he was there but had given me the reins to go forward. I felt deep in my soul that if things got to be too much for me, he would step in. But, for now, I knew I was in charge. So I made plans for the kids and their schools. I had to go and speak with both schools and let them know what was happening and that I wasn't sure how the kids were going to handle it. I told them I knew they might have a few rough days and I needed them to understand. McKynna had the best first-grade teacher we could have ever imagined. So amazing how God sets it all up on all levels. I not only had the best medical team I could have ever hoped for but my children were also blessed with the people the Lord surrounded them with. It was the worst situation, but somehow I had peace in a lot of ways. Again, the Lord doing his thing.

CHAPTER FORTY

So things with the kids were settled, and I had to make the call I was dreading. Being a part of Southwest Airlines is unlike anything else. Southwest Airlines is more than just a place to work. It is our family away from our biological families. When you are hired, you are made to know that you are special and will always be treated as such. They let you know that you are chosen for a reason. Herb, Colleen, and Gary our leaders, have always said we were hired for our uniqueness. We are taught that each one of us brings our own little bit of magic to Southwest Airlines. They have always said they can teach anyone a skill but can't teach you to be *you*. Special has to come from the heart. The day I received my wings to fly with this amazing family was the day my life changed forever. When they gave me my wings, it was not only to soar on the airplane but in life. I was blessed the day they took a chance on me, and I have known what I have been a part of ever since. I have never taken a day at Southwest for granted.

I was in management for several years and have dealt with a lot of people who needed help. I never thought I would be one of the people calling and needing to ask for support. Unfortunately I would have to make that call. I put it off as long as I could, and the time had come to tell them I was sick and that I would need some Southwest love. They were so great and wanted to help me in every way possible. I felt more love than I ever imagined. Before I knew it, they stepped up and went to work for me. It was exactly the feeling I needed right at that very moment. I let them know that I didn't have a lot to tell them as of yet. I had to have my first surgery, and then I would be back in touch with more details. I remember hanging up the phone and sitting on the edge of the bed crying and not believing this was my life. I loved my job second to my family, and I was going to fight for it. It was the best job in the universe—and still is, by the way. I can honestly tell you I wouldn't be here sharing my story with you without my Southwest Airlines family. I wasn't only staying here on this earth for my babies but also because I would be back in the air and on that plane. It gave me a purpose and another big reason not to leave this earth yet.

About a week went by, and I got a phone call from the Dallas office. It was a sweet friend of mine, and she had heard about what was going on. She gave me some really great words of encouragement. Then she led into the fact that I hadn't filled out my paperwork for my leave. I let her know I had no intentions of taking a leave.

She said, "Oh, Christi, you will have to take a leave."

I said, "Well, if I take a leave, will you still have to take my badge?"

She said, "Yes, but you get it back as soon as your doctor releases you."

I said, "That is what I thought." I went on to inform her I would not be taking a leave. I told her I was going to give all my trips away like I had been and I would make it work.

She said, "Christi, do you understand that you are going to be under a lot of care and you might miss a deadline?" She insisted I take the leave.

I told her I had to know psychologicly that I had much more work to do here in this beautiful world and being a part of Southwest Airlines was at the top of my list. I explained to her that taking my badge was not an option. It would be taking my "WINGS" away. I had to know that I had a job to go back to. I told her I wasn't going to give it up unless the Lord took me. I let her know I was going to look at my Southwest badge and my wings daily to remind me of where I would be again. I was a part of that family, and nothing was going to take that away from me. I made her see it was much more than what met the eye. Southwest wasn't just a job. Next to my children, it was my purpose.

By the end of the conversation, she completely got where I was coming from and said, "I love you, and promise you will call me if you need anything."

I made her a promise and thanked her from the bottom of my heart for her understanding. She had no idea how much the support she gave me helped to give me great strength to move forward and know I was doing the right thing. I had such an outpour of coworkers call and send me gifts, cards, and encouragement to give me strength.

That was what we were taught at Southwest: We help each other no matter what. The strong help the weak. Do unto others as you would have them do unto you. That was always one of the most valuable things spoken to us; internally for employees and externally for customers. That was how we treated one another. I had never needed it until now, and all of what Colleen, had instilled in us held true. My Southwest family stepped up, and I couldn't believe all the love and support I received. We truly are the LUV airline. Without it I would never have made it. Not in a million years. So I felt at that moment I had a lot of extra support that I so desperately needed. It was a defining moment for me that revealed what I was really a part of. I was a part of one the most dedicated and loving companies ever created. I know our success at Southwest Airlines is because we truly dedicate ourselves to one another. We do it without trying. It is second nature to our employees, and we do it without merit. I survived because of the people and the benefits provided by Southwest Airlines. My insurance was a Godsend. I didn't have to worry about my care or money. I know that was a huge part of my survival. I could think about getting well and not how I was going to afford it or that my job was in jeopardy. I was a part of something more special than I ever realized.

CHAPTER FORTY ONE

My surgery date was a few days away, and it was time to sit down and explain to my little ones that Mommy was about to go to the hospital and get better. I had no idea what I was going to say to them. All I knew was that I asked God to bring the words to me and to help them feel safe that everything was going to be all right. I needed to make them believe with all their little hearts that Mommy was going to be as good as new. I wanted them to know that no matter what happened I would be all right and back to normal very soon. So I sat them both down and told them that Nana would be staying and taking care of them while Mommy's boo-boos were healing. I let them know they were going to be big boo-boos and that it would take a while for them to heal. Of course, McKynna was my big girl, and I told her I was going to need her help when I came home from the hospital. She was very excited thinking she was going to be my nurse. They took it amazingly, and I wanted to keep it very simple. I didn't want to cloud their little brains with anything difficult. I think I did a great job, and they were good with what was about to happen. McKynna being only six and McGraw only four,

I needed to be brief and confident with them. I have learned that sometimes they are smarter than we are.

So I think I was ready. I had talked to everyone and tried to make all arrangements I could before the big day. I flew Andrew's brother in. I was very close to him. I always had been. Jason had a softer side to him, and I had always had a good relationship with him. I was glad he was coming. I was hoping it would help Andrew a bit.

It was still a few days out from my surgery, and we had a buyer on the house. Andrew knew we needed to sell it, but it wasn't a great deal. It was killing him to think he would have to settle.

I had been talking to Rae on and off. Everything with her mom had been keeping her busy. She had so much going on, dealing with the loss of her mom, I didn't want to make her life any more cloudy than it already was. I missed her with every fiber of my being. I wanted her to be there with me so bad, but I knew she couldn't. I would call her right before I went in and have my mom call her after I was out.

I had made most of my calls and did everything I had to do. All I had left was to say my prayers and try to get some rest for what would be the single most important day of my life. I was ready even if I wasn't. I wanted it to get out of my body. It had been in there for so long. I had to really turn it over for now and know that it would be what it would be. It was out of my hands. I had trusted in God and made my decisions, and now I had to follow through.

CHAPTER FORTY TWO

I was so cold I couldn't get warm to save my life. My nerves were so bad that I stayed cold and couldn't quit shaking. I talked to God and told him we were the A team and it was going to be great. I knew together we would conquer this. Andrew, Mom, and Jason all came back with me while they got me prepped. I said my good-byes to my babies and told them Mommy would be back and they were going to help me get better. They told me they would say lots of prayers for me. I think the hardest part was letting go of them and knowing I would not be able to help them during this time even if I wanted to. I had to let go and focus on getting that evil out of my body so I wouldn't have to say good-bye forever. That was the reality.

Everyone was so nice and took very good care of me. They were a team I couldn't have picked on my own if I tried. I found Dr. Christopher through Dr. Wynn. When I went to him to talk about the reconstruction of my breast, I was timid and embarrassed. I found myself at his mercy to make me look normal again. I made him understand how important it was for me to look as close to my original self. I told him to do what he had to in order to make it happen. He was so classy and kind and assured me he would give it his all. I shed many tears in his office, and he was very understanding and full of grace. I saw both doctors in my room right before my surgery. I felt a calmness come over me. Between God and my team, I couldn't lose.

So they came and rolled me into my room. I cried the entire time. I was terrified and ready for it to be done. I remember them looking at me and saying, "All right, Christi, here we go. Let's do this." I remember saying OK, and that was it.

I woke up in the recovery room and didn't remember anything. I was really groggy and felt terrible. I went back to sleep, and the next thing I knew I was in my own room. I am not really sure how long I was in there when I finally woke up. I was so medicated I could barely focus on anything in the room. Prior to the surgery, Andrew and I had talked, and I told him I didn't want the kids to see me in a bad state. I asked him not to bring them around me until I was somewhat normal. The last thing I wanted was for them to ever be scared of me or think I was going to die. They were so little, and I didn't want them to suffer more than necessary. I was their safe place, and I wanted them to always feel that. I remember barely waking up and being so medicated.

I was so out of it, and I will never forget trying to focus on who was in the room when I opened my eyes. The first person I saw was my mom, and I also saw my dear friend Katherine.

I felt so bad, and my stomach was feeling so sick from all the medicine. I just wanted to rest. I was hurting so bad that the nurse came in and gave me my medicine and I went right back to sleep for the night. It was just me and my mom that stayed. Andrew took the kids home and stayed with them for the night. They weren't used to being with him alone. I was always with them, and if I wasn't, my mom was. It was a good thing I went to sleep and didn't know what was going on. Andrew's brother stayed with them at the hotel, and they loved being with him. They kept me really medicated throughout the night to help me rest.

I woke the next morning, and my mom was right by my side. I didn't know anything the doctors had told them, so I was ready to hear what they had found. I needed to know if the cancer had gotten into my lymph nodes. I would never forgive myself if they did. I mean because I didn't go to the doctor as early as I should have, and if it had traveled, I would not be able to handle it. When I was able to focus and listen to the doctors, they came in to talk to me. They had removed four nodes on my cancer side and two on the other. They also removed the cancer and got everything they could out to try to keep it from coming back. They said the surgery went well and my lymph nodes were all negative. It hadn't spread, and it was a little out of the tumor. I am convinced without a shadow of a doubt that without the insight God gave me I wouldn't be here sharing my journey. The instinct that God instilled in me and the feeling I had are the only reason I am alive today.

It was a relief, and now the healing would begin. It was worse than I thought. I had drain tubes, and I hurt more than I ever thought possible. I am not complaining because it was worth all of it. I would do it one hundred times if it meant being able to raise my babies. I had to figure out how to live my life normally with my drain tubes and the pain. I was only down for a few days before I was right back to my daily routine. I knew my chemo road was nearing, and I wanted to make our days as normal as ever. I didn't know what was going to happen after I started my chemo, so I wanted to make the most of this time. They let me know I would have to take four rounds of precautionary chemotherapy. My cancer was so aggressive that they wanted to be extra sure there wasn't any floating around in my body. And I said from the beginning that I was going to do whatever they said and whatever they felt was best. I started to learn early on they had a protocol; however, I could tell it wasn't always one size fits all. I was learning what worked for some didn't necessarily work for all. Nevertheless I was going to do it all to survive.

I was very grateful that going into this I was healthy. I had been so good to my body during my life, and now it was going to pay off. It would help me recover and get me back on my feet a lot quicker. For that I was extremely grateful. I felt so very blessed for the great outcome of my surgery, and now I needed to get stronger for my next hurdle. It would not only be physical but also extremely mental for me. I was struggling to keep a smile on my face. I hurt so badly and was so scared. The unknown once again was a lot to swallow. I didn't care anything about how sick I would feel. I have to be honest that the most important thing for me was how I would end up looking after it was all over. I already felt like I looked like a war zone. I had huge scars I was trying to take care of, and I knew that was just the beginning. I was having so many weak moments. I tried to stay strong and not listen to the voices. It was hard, and they would take me over in my exhausted moments. My faith was strong, but the negative thoughts would creep in and take my mind over. I would literally get on my knees and beg God to take them away. I told him I was stronger than this and I needed him to hold me and let me know I was going to beat this.

I had been getting out even when I didn't feel like it. It was hard to secure the drains to where no one could see them. I was bound and determined to live a normal life and do for my children as I always had. The Lord was with me day in and day out. I felt him near me always. Sometimes I would think I was taking up all of his time. I will say he knew I needed to feel his presence, and some days it was like he let me know every second he was there.

One afternoon my mom and I went to Walmart. It was time to buy Easter goodies, and I wanted to get it done before my rounds of chemo started. I wanted to be a part of it and had no idea how I was going to feel in the coming weeks. McGraw loved white chocolate bunnies. They were his favorite, and to be honest that was all he really wanted in his basket. I was looking around the Easter candy and couldn't find one anywhere. While I was looking around, I noticed this beautiful girl dressed in a cute tennis skirt and with a hat to cover her head. She was bald, and I could tell she had already started her journey. I was so intrigued by her and stayed close to her while shopping. I knew she could tell I was watching her, and she was so very sweet. For some reason I felt very close to her, and I didn't know why. I really thought it was because I was about to lose my hair and she looked so much like me. I was trying to grasp any closeness to it that I could. I know in my heart that God places everything in our paths for a specific reason. It is all in perfect timing. We are all meant to meet each other for one reason or another, good or bad. I know she was in that Walmart and looking at Easter merchandise for a reason, and that reason was me.

I guess she had overheard me and my mom talking, and she walked up and said, "Is this what you are looking for?" She then handed me a large white chocolate bunny. "I overheard what you were searching for, and I think this is it."

I looked at her and literally started crying. I was emotional already, and for her to make an effort like that was unfathomable. It's funny. It's like God knows whom to give the battles to. I think he handpicks us and knows without a shadow of a doubt we will use it for the good. We will take our challenge and heartache and inspire those who can't do it on their own. I would come to know that Shannon was that person. I literally went to Walmart that day reluctantly. I was hurting and feeling down but knew I needed to get out. Who would have thought I would have found a guardian angel that day at Walmart? I said I was sorry and asked her if I could talk to her.

She said, "About my cancer?"

I said, "Yes, is that all right?"

She looked at me and gave me the warmest smile I have ever felt in my life. I mean I had this feeling come over me like you wouldn't believe. No words to describe it. I felt God was standing right there with the two of us to make sure we stayed right there until our relationship was solid. It happened so fast, and my entire outlook changed.

I said, "Hi, my name is Christi."

She said, "Hello, Christi, my name is Shannon. What would you like to know?"

I said, "Well, I would like to know about your chemotherapy experience."

She looked at me with a puzzled look and said, "Of course. Why do you ask?"

I told her that I had breast cancer and I would be undergoing chemotherapy soon. I told her I had just gotten my double mastectomy and tested positive for the BRCA1 cancer gene. I explained it was passed on to me by my father's side. I could tell when I was talking to her that something was changing in her demeanor. I couldn't put my finger on it, and I told her I was sorry if it was too much information. I was desperate to prepare myself for my road ahead. I will never forget what came out of her mouth.

Shannon looked at me and said, "No, it's all right. You aren't going to believe this. I have the same gene and have been going through the same process."

I couldn't believe my ears. I know we were looking at each other like we were both ghosts. I looked at her and said, "I am sorry. What did you say? You have the BRCA1 gene?"

Shannon looked at me and said, "Yes, I do.

I asked, "Double mastectomy? Left breast? Four rounds of precautionary chemotherapy? And did you have a hysterectomy too?"

When she replied yes to all of the above, I almost literally threw up on the floor. We were in fact the same people in different bodies. We began to share information and stories, and I couldn't believe it. I don't even have words to tell you how we both felt at that moment. It truly was a defining moment in my life and in my journey regarding my understanding of faith. I had never felt the presence of God in my life more than at that very moment. I knew that Shannon and I had been chosen for this journey for many reasons. I knew we were special and God wanted us to know we weren't on the journey alone. I mean he wanted us to make it clear that we had work to do in this world and we were going to help each other do it. The chances of someone having exactly what I had in the same location were just one in a million. And I was standing next to that person in my Walmart at that very moment. I was in awe of all that had just taken place. I knew I would travel my road very differently from this moment on. It gave me a completely different vision of how I was going to get through this hell. Because let me say it was literally hell I was living. And I wanted out. For the first time, I started looking at my cancer as a savior and not a death sentence. Meeting Shannon, having her by my side, and sharing all that she had gone through made it doable. God makes a way when there isn't one. I finally realized I was at the center of this for many reasons in my life as well as for many others. I would pave the way for many in my life. I promised God I would do the work he needed me to do with my best ability. I knew he wouldn't leave my side now and forever. It gave me this calm sense that I was going to do this and after I was done I was going to help others too. This was my life for now, and it was my choice how I was going to get through it. So I decided at that moment I would be getting through it with a smile. I wanted to be an example of how there is life after cancer and it doesn't have to mean death. I owned it and was ready to move on and get it all done.

CHAPTER FORTY TWO

I had already done my double mastectomy, and now it was chemo time. On the subject of hair loss, I have a different view than some. I am going to tell on myself a little by saying that hair isn't just hair to me. My hair has always been a big part of my world. I love hair so much that straight out of high school after graduation I moved to San Antonio with my high-school sweetheart. Greg was going to attend college at UTSA, and my plan was to attend cosmetology school. I had wanted to do that since I could remember. I loved hair and always stayed up on the latest and greatest. It was all working out like clockwork, and then one day we had to start actually taking clients and touching real people's hair—and I really had a phobia about it. I loved hair and doing hair, just not for people I didn't know. I know: so crazy, and even crazier that I dropped out and had to make another career choice. Greg couldn't believe it simply because I had talked about it for years. So hair goes way back for me.

And now facing the fact that my identity was being taken away from me was completely unfathomable. I would stare at myself and brush my hair endlessly. I didn't bring it up to the kids until I felt they were feeling better about my surgery. I had so many phases of my treatment that I had to pace it with them. They were babies, and I knew how hard it was for me to grasp it, much less them. So I finally decided the day I was going to sit them down and really share with them the side effects of the medicine that Mommy was going to start taking. You have to understand that the side effects of the chemotherapy affect us all. I would feel it differently because it was my body, but loved ones such as my children and my parents would feel it in another way. Very devastating to all involved. So it was really important the way I shared this with them. It would be the hardest conversation I would have with anyone to date, even harder than the one when I told them I was sick.

I sat them both down and told them it was time for Mommy to start taking her medicine. I let them know I would have to go to the doctor to take it and then I could come back home. I let them know the medicine was going to make Mommy feel very sick in her tummy. They understood that because they'd had tummy aches. They could relate to it. Then I went on to tell them that Mommy would get bigger. I said I would slowly get bigger and would have to start buying bigger clothes. I think I was more worried about that part. But a small price to pay to live. I knew I could try hard, work out, and hope I wouldn't gain too much. Then the only other big thing was my hair. My heart was pounding, and I looked at them and said, "All right, there is only one more thing I need to tell you. The medicine it so strong that it will make Mommy lose her hair."

McGraw had this puzzled look on his face, and McKynna said, "Mommy, you are going to be bald?"

My eyes filled with tears, and I said, "I am afraid so, baby. All of it will be gone."

Her eyes filled up, and she said, "Oh, Mommy, I am so sorry."

I put my face in my hands and cried. All of a sudden, I felt this little hand on my hair. I looked up, and it was my boy.

He said, "Don't cry, Mommy."

They both told me that no matter what I was still the best mommy in the world. I knew right then I needed to let it go and we would deal with it when it happened. And, besides, maybe I would be one of the few that it wouldn't happen to. I could pray for that and see what happened. The kids were my rock, and I just focused on them until the time arrived.

I was taking so many pills and trying to keep it all straight. I went from not even taking Tylenol to taking the entire drugstore. It was all so overwhelming, and I was so thankful for my family and friends. I had more support being in a new city than I could have ever imagined. I was blessed beyond measure. I will never forget the morning of my first treatment. McGraw had grown very clingy since my surgery, and he could feel that his mommy wasn't all right. His preschool called us daily, and I had to go get him early almost everyday. I made the decision to pull him out. Now McKynna was struggling bad in school. She couldn't focus and was scared as well. She missed her mommy being that vibrant person she had always known. As hard as I tried, some days McKynna knew I wasn't good. She was older, and it truly affected her more intensely. I knew she was struggling in her class, but I felt it better for her to be at school with her friends. So I had to take McGraw to the cancer center with us. He would be there for my first treatment. It made me nervous and glad at the same time. I loved that I could look at his precious face but didn't want him to be scared for life. My mom was absolutely the best with him and helped keep him busy. He knew Mommy was taking medicine and then we could all go home.

The experience of my first treatment was chilling. I went in and couldn't believe I was going to have to do it. I was going to have to take poison to stay alive. It was all so contradictory. I was in it to live. I dressed for success because I knew if I felt pretty and successful, I would be successful. I would stop at nothing to make sure I stayed Christi.

I sat down in the chair, and they asked me if I was ready.

I said, "Ready as I will ever be."

My doctor came in, went over it all with me, and said, "Let's do this."

They gave me so much medicine even before they gave me my chemo. I just couldn't believe it. The process was exhausting as well as the drugs. I was in there most of the day.

By the time I was finished, I didn't think I could even make it home. It was all a blur, and I just wanted to rest. I took my medicines and went to bed. I remember waking the next morning thinking I was going to feel sick and not be able to get out of bed. Well, I guess I did feel queasy and weak, but it was nothing I couldn't handle. I can remember being so excited knowing I was going to be able to take McKynna to school and be normal. I can remember wondering every minute of the day if the side effects were going to kick in. It was all a waiting game. I had three weeks until my next treatment, and I was so glad. It would give me time to become mentally prepared to go at it again. I could already tell my hair was starting to thin. I couldn't believe it. One round of that evil stuff, and it was already taking my hair from me. It was like it had a mind of its own and no mercy. I would wake up in the morning, and hair would be all over my pillow. It was hard for me to even go to sleep because I was scared I would wake up and it would all be gone. I had nightmares about it every night. I really had so much anxiety about my hair I would lie down and try to not fall asleep so I could make sure I wouldn't lose one strand.

One morning I woke up, and on one side of my head, the hair was almost all the way gone. I remember when I went into the bathroom and looked in the mirror, my heart sank. I sat down on the side of the bathtub in our hotel room and sobbed like a baby. It was then and there that I knew it would all have to come off. I said from the beginning that I would shave it off if it began to get bald spots all over. I didn't want to look like that. I had made up my mind my hair would all come off that day while the kids were at school. I didn't want them to know anything about it until it was done, and I had figured out how to wear my wigs and wear them well. I mean I wanted them to look like the real deal. I had looked on the Internet for the perfect ones, and I found them. When they arrived, they looked amazing. I mean they looked so real it was scary. I couldn't have been more pleased. I would wear them and wear them well.

So everything was in place, and all I had to do was shave it off. I had thought about going to a salon and having it done. But then I would have to walk out and would also have others sitting around me. None of that was all right with me, and I just couldn't do it. It was something so personal that I had to do it alone. If I could have done it myself, I would have. I tried to figure out a way, but it wouldn't work. So my only option was to have someone do it for me in the privacy of my hotel room. I knew my mom couldn't handle it, so I asked Andrew to do the honors. He was glad to do it. I was grateful he was going to help me, and who better to help me than my husband? So we had all of the supplies we needed and were ready. I was struggling mentally, but it was time to get it done so I could focus on getting well. I will never forget the entire process. I didn't want to look in the mirror while it was being done. So I looked in the mirror before it was done. Andrew stood behind me, and I took a deep breath and asked God to put his hands on me and give me all the strength I would need. God knew how much I would need. I would have rather taken twenty rounds of chemo than lose my hair. It wasn't just hair. It was my hair and my security. I had already lost my two pretty breasts, if you don't mind me saying. And now I was going to be losing the only other thing I liked on my body. So I told Andrew to do it quickly and get it done. I didn't need a gentle touch. I just needed it off, and I was glad Andrew was doing it because his personality was just right for the job.

As the first few hairs started to fall, so did my body. I can honestly tell you that made me feel a million times sicker than the chemo had. There was no turning back, and my hair would be gone for God knew how long. It was that moment of truth when I had to actually look in the mirror and learn who I was. I knew I was changed forever and I had to get comfortable with this person I had just turned into. I knew if I didn't, I would never make the entire journey, and I was in it to win it. I was going to beat this and with flying colors. So I needed Andrew to give me some time alone. He tried to the best of his ability to help me, and I appreciated it, but I had to get through this on my own. I had to do this my own way. I had to mourn and suffer in my own way and then figure out how I was going to pick myself up and move forward.

As I got up from the bathtub and looked at myself for the first time, it was a time of truth. My illness was real, but the key was making sure it didn't define me. I couldn't believe that was me. I was so scared and repulsed that I threw up in the sink. I stood there and cried and didn't even care that I was a mess. I put my head in my hands and let out the biggest scream. I knew I was sick and thought to myself, are you kidding me? For the first time, I looked up and yelled at God, "Why me? Why me? What did I do that was so very bad that you did this to me?" I had told myself from the very beginning I would always stand in faith, and I knew that God was my partner in this journey, but at this moment I was angry and bitter. I was mad at everyone, including God. I knew we should never ask why; however, at this moment I couldn't control my thoughts or my words. I sat on that cold bathroom floor covered in yuck and without hair and wept. That was all I knew to do right then. I had no strength to fight and to be honest didn't even want to fight. I wanted to feel sorry for myself. I had no idea right then if I would even get my fight back. I had never felt so helpless in my entire life. I mean to the point of not feeling anything at all. I can remember my mom trying to help me and Andrew trying to give me words of encouragement, and I didn't want any part of it. For the first time, I was so mad that I didn't care. All I could do was sit there and think about what was taken from me. Christi was taken from me, and it felt like someone sucked every bit of who and what I was out of my body. How would I get past this? After all, I repulsed myself and couldn't imagine what I would do to others.

My mom was beside herself, and I can't even imagine how she must have felt. I was her baby, and she had to see me go through chemo hell. I know she hurt more than I hurt. I remember wondering how I was ever going to face my children. I had all these questions in my mind. They were babies, and the last thing I wanted was for them to be scared and not even recognize their own mommy. I have no idea how long I sat on that floor. It was one of the most humiliating moments of my life.

I finally let my mom into the bathroom, and she held me and let me cry for what felt like forever. She didn't say a word but just let me feel everything I was feeling. I don't think I could have made it through that day without that time with her. I knew she was dying for me and there was nothing she could do. I had hit rock bottom, and she had too. I know she felt everything I felt. I will never forget asking her if she thought I would ever be pretty again. I looked at her and asked her why this happened to me. I looked at her and said I was sorry for anything I had ever done that made God so mad at me that he would give this to me.

I will never forget the look on her face. She looked at me and said, "Baby, you didn't do anything. God didn't give this to you because you were bad."

We both sat on that cold bathroom floor and cried. I finally was so exhausted from crying that I changed my clothes and just wanted to rest. I wanted my mom to lie with me and hold me like when I was little. I finally fell asleep and got some rest.

When I woke up, I thought it might have been a dream, and then when I reached up and felt the top of my head, I knew it was real. I started to cry and felt so very sad. My mom came and sat on the side of the bed and said the kids would be home soon and we had to prepare for them. I knew I was going to have to put on another performance and not show them my sadness. It was already so hard on them that I couldn't let them down. So I dried my tears and told my mom to get my wig that looked just like my hair. It was about my children now, not me. No matter the reason I was sitting there with cancer and all my hair gone, the fact of the matter was it was what it was. It wasn't my babies' fault, and they should feel nothing I was feeling. There was no more time for self-pity. My children were coming home, and I needed to get it together.

I pulled the wig out of the box, and I was burning all over my body with anxiety. I had to make myself look like their mommy. I went to the mirror and tried to figure out how to put it on. I worked with it for a while and fixed it the best I could. I knew it was going to take practice, but I was going to master it and would make sure my kids wouldn't know until I was ready. I wanted it on my terms. Since my son was breastfed, he would play with my hair while he was falling asleep every night. I was not ready to change his routine. I wanted to feel close to my children. Putting my babies to sleep was so special, and I wanted everything to stay the same. I figured until I was ready I would wear my wig until they were asleep and then take it off to sleep. It was the only thing I could think of. I had already told them I would be losing my hair. I knew McGraw didn't understand, but McKynna did. I wasn't ready to tell them that it already happened. I still couldn't believe that it was already gone after one treatment. I had so much hair, and it was unbelievable that it was gone. So I wanted to get a grasp on it myself before I told them. So I was going to wear my wig until they were asleep, and I would set my alarm and be up and have it on before they woke up. I figured this would work for a while. My hair coming out was the worst symptom, and it happened so fast. I thought it was going to be really bad and that I would be sicker than I was. I did remember that Shannon told me it would get worse with every treatment. But I will say I was happy I was feeling all right for the moment.

CHAPTER FORTY THREE

So before I knew it, I was already headed back up to the cancer center for my second treatment. I was on a three-week schedule, and those first three weeks flew by. Once again I did the same thing, making sure I dressed beautifully and trying to make my wig look great so no one would know I had already lost my hair. It all happened so fast, and I couldn't believe I had already lost it and was only going in for my second treatment. One treatment was all it took. So when I entered the cancer center for the second time, I truly felt like I belonged there. I knew I was sick like the others. My family was with me, and McGraw came with us too. I will never forget how having him there brought calmness over me. I wanted him to be with me, and he wanted to be with me as well.

When they called my name, once again I was so scared, and we all walked back to my room. I was always in the same room, and the same nurses were assigned to me. It did help me with being a little more comfortable, and it was good I had a routine. So we were all in my room, and my oncologist came in and went over how I was feeling. She asked me questions, and we talked about my progress. I let her know I had already lost my hair and could talk freely because my mom had McGraw and was getting him a snack. I wanted him to be settled when we got started. When they came back in the room, my mom and Andrew were both in there with me. McGraw was sitting in his chair, and I was watching him, trying to keep my mind off of that poison they were once again about to pour into my body.

The nurse came in, sat down by me, and said, "We have to talk."

My heart sank. I had no idea what she was about to tell me. She looked at me with the saddest face and told me that McGraw would not be able to stay with me in the room. She said it was just not good for all of the patients. I understood but started to cry, and so did McGraw. We both had thought we were doing this together. My heart broke for the two of us. I had to explain it to him, and he had no idea why he couldn't stay. My mom took him out of the room, and I sat and cried. Andrew said he would take him and get him something to eat while I was getting my treatment. They did everything, giving me all my premeds and getting me ready. I was tired before they even started. I wanted it to just be over.

So they started my treatment, and Mom sat in there with me. I can remember positioning my chair by the window so I could see out. I got so tired of looking at the depressing things inside the rooms that I wanted to see outside. It was still so cold outside, and the window was kind of fogged up. I remembered Andrew had said he was taking McGraw to the big hospital to eat. Besides his favorite nurse Julie in Dr. Wynn's office, the only other thing he really liked was the turkey sandwich in the hospital cafeteria. He called Julie his favorite girl. I loved him so very much, and he was like me because he found good in all the bad. Even little things made him happy. I was looking out the window and saw them coming across the street in the cold. My boy looked so sweet and happy. When he got closer to the cancer center, I could tell he was looking for something. He walked to the front of the center, and I couldn't see him anymore. All of a sudden, I looked up, and he was walking around looking in the windows to find me. It was cold, and the sun was trying to come out. I asked Mom "What he was doing?"

She looked at me and said, "I think he is looking for you."

I said, "What?" and about that time his little face was looking in my window. "Oh, McGraw, I see you."

We were both so happy, and he got to see his mama after all. I looked at him through the window, and tears were coming from my eyes. I couldn't believe he actually found me. He was so smart and persistent. Then he did something I will never forget. I could tell he was so very sad he couldn't be in there with me, and he started to cry. He then put his little hand on the window and held it there until I put my hand on the window. I have never seen him so happy. He had found his mommy, and he knew I was all right. It was so cold outside, and he didn't even care. I looked at him with tears streaming down, and I mouthed to him that I loved him. My sweet angel wasn't leaving his mommy, and I wasn't about to leave him. From that moment on, I was in this, and I was going to beat it. I knew at that very moment my children would do what it took to see me and be near me, and I would do the same for them. We were the breath of one another, and I would not take that from them. This wasn't fair to them, and they didn't deserve to live without me. So from that Chemo treatment moving forward, I was a different person.

We finished up that day, and I felt really tired after. I knew it would start getting harder, but that was when I had to start getting stronger. I had no time for weakness. So a few days went by, and I won't lie that I felt a lot worse. I hadn't told the kids yet about my hair so I had to make sure I kept my wig on and still looked like their mommy. It was so hard to even have the strength to get up, dress, and take McKynna to school. I knew I would have to tell them and tell them soon about my hair. I wasn't going to be able to hide it much longer.

It was getting harder by the day. I wasn't sleeping well knowing I had to wake up every morning, put my wig on, and act like I was still the same mommy they had always known. McKynna had started to ask me a few questions about my hair, and I knew it was only a matter of time. Our vacation was coming up, and I knew I was going to have to tell them before the trip. My heart was so sad because I knew that just as it was for me this would be a defining moment for them. Mommy as they knew her wasn't the same, and I didn't know when she would be back. I was so terrified to tell them because I didn't want to scare them. So that evening, I decided it would be that night. I wanted it to be done so we could all get used to the fact that I was bald.

I had them come into the room, and I am telling you I had the worst feeling in the pit of my stomach. I had no idea how I was going to tell them, and as hard as I tried, you can't rehearse something like that. So I had them both in front of me, and I told them Mommy had something very important to tell them. I told them since we were going to Orlando on vacation soon, there was something Mommy had to do before we left. I tried to keep it together because I knew if I cried, they would too. I started letting them know that I was doing well and that Mommy was feeling good enough to go on our vacation. I asked them to go back and think about when Mommy had sat them down and talked to them about what could happen to Mommy when she took her medicine. McGraw did exactly as I knew he would: he looked at me like he had no idea what I was talking about. And of course McKynna knew exactly what I was talking about. She looked at me with the most scared look on her face, and my eyes filled with tears.

I looked at her and said, "It's all right, baby girl. It is all going to be all right. Mommy is going to look different for a while, but I will be all right, and one day I will look normal again."

I looked at her, and she started to cry. Her beautiful blue eyes poured tears for me and for her. McGraw had no idea what was wrong, and I knew the only way was to show him. I had my wig on, and the moment that I would have to share their new mommy with them had come. I was so very scared that my children wouldn't even want to be around me.

So I took a deep breath and told them, "I am going to show you what the bad medicine has done to Mommy."

I reached up, pulled off my wig, and told them that for a while this would be what Mommy would look like. I was trying not to cry but couldn't help myself. I felt like in a lot of ways I had let my children down. I was supposed to be the one person in their lives that was the strongest and they could lean on no matter what. How could I do that if they were scared of me? When I took off my wig, my daughter could not believe her eyes. I saw her take the biggest gasp, and my son was very confused.

McGraw walked over to me and said, "Mommy, is that you?"

I said, "Yes, baby, it is. The medicine made Mommy's hair fall out sooner than she thought." I looked at him. "I am so very sorry, McGraw."

He reached up and touched my head, and then he turned around and went to go play with his toys. McKynna sat there with me and just stared at me for a while. I knew she was sad for me. We sat there and cried together. I could tell she was very uncomfortable and didn't really want to talk about it any longer. Sitting here writing about it is almost unbearable. I knew at that moment my daughter would not be the same with me for a while. They both went to watch television, and I can remember sitting there and sobbing in my hands. I was no longer that beautiful, strong mommy they knew. Reality was that I knew I wouldn't be that mommy again for a long time. I had no idea how to get past this and move forward.

I put my wig back on and decided to go for a walk in the hotel. I had to clear my head and talk to God. The only way to get through something like this is to truly ask him for his help. I needed his hand to guide me to a stronger place. I know it sounds crazy, but when I lost my hair, I lost more than hair. I lost my strength and my confidence, and I needed it back. I knew I wasn't going to be able to get back without the help of God. I understand there are a lot of people who have doubts about God or a higher being. I had always been raised to know God would take care of us.

But knowing that he is there if you need him and actually needing him are two completely different things. When you actually have to rely on him and put your life in his hands, it's a different ball game. Turning over your complete trust to someone we can't see and can't get actual feedback from is incomprehensible. I wish I could sit here and tell you that I didn't have any doubts and that I knew for certain he was going to keep me here in this world, but I would be lying. It took every bit of energy I had to know that he had my back. Walking around that hotel fighting for my life and feeling vulnerable in every sense of the word, I did what I had to do. I will be honest and tell you turning it over to him took every bit of my energy.

I had the worst kind of cancer, not to mention a genetic mark against me. All the odds weren't in my favor. So I would love to tell you I was comfortable and knew he would see me through. But that isn't the truth at all. It is easy to believe and be supportive in your religion when things are going right in your life. It is when everything that you have ever known hangs in the balance—like whether you will live to watch your children grow into their own lives—that you question everything you thought you believed in. I carried a lot of guilt for a very long time because I was not as real with God as I should have been. I waited until I was hanging on by a thread to submerge myself in him.

So after a lot of guilt and many apologies to God, I decided I was worth saving. Even though I wasn't the perfect Christian and I wasn't always living his way, I knew he had my hand, and I begged him and told him he wouldn't be sorry if he allowed me to stay here.

So after about an hour of walking around and searching my soul, I went back to my room, got my kids, and made sure they knew that Mommy would be back. I told them I would be back better than ever. They both knew I meant it, and I could tell the more confident I was with myself, the better they felt. It sounds so easy, but it was so very hard to stay strong and confident for my children.

CHAPTER FORTY FOUR

We were all so excited about vacation. It was so needed, and the kids had their sweet minds on something other than Mommy being sick. So we packed all of our things and headed to Orlando. I loved it there, and I hoped and prayed I would feel free from it all for a week. It was great that I had two treatments down and only two to go when I got back. I was hoping to get my second wind for the last two treatments and a tan. I thought being tan and bald would be better than being pale and bald. I was trying everything to make up for my hair being gone.

    I knew that Andrew needed to get away too. Things were really heavy with the selling of our house and his job. I didn't see him smile often. I had been feeling very distant from him and was hoping this trip would help. I will never forget when we were sitting on the plane waiting to take off and Andrew's phone rang. I had to sit in front of him because I had the kids. I looked back, and he was smiling and talking to someone who changed his attitude completely. I hadn't seen him smile that much in a very long time. I waited until he got off the phone and asked him what the call was about. He looked at me, smiled really big, and said they found another buyer for the house. I couldn't believe it. I was so excited for him and for our family. I had prayed for that every day so that maybe we could move out of the hotel and get a condo or apartment. I was so excited because I knew when we got back, we could move and I could finish out my treatments in the privacy of a home of our own. In one phone call, the tone of our trip changed completely. I said a quiet prayer to myself and thanked God from the bottom of my heart for blessing us with a buyer. I know he knew I needed less stress, and this would do it.

So on to Orlando we went, and we were all ready to be with family and have a great time. The trip was better than I thought. It was the first time I had seen Andrew's side of the family since my diagnosis, and I had no idea what to expect. It was all right, and everyone treated me as normally as they could. It was extremely hot, and I wore my wig as much as possible. I tried to act like it wasn't bothering me and I was all right. I really didn't want any of Andrew's family to see that I didn't have it all together. I tried to keep it together and not show any emotions. By the middle of the week, I just couldn't take it anymore. I was hot and miserable, and I didn't want to let on to the kids that their much-awaited trip to Florida wasn't so magical. I wanted it to be about them and not about me. It was one of those things where if I took my wig off and went natural, it would be a big deal and all attention would be on me, whereas if I didn't and left it on, I was irritable. It was a no-win situation. So I decided to talk to McKynna and see how she felt about my taking it off and wearing a ball cap the rest of the trip. I couldn't hold my tears back when I brought her in our room to discuss it with her. I think I scared her a little and it took her by surprise. But I told her I needed her to be a big girl and help Mommy make a big decision. I also let her know that how she felt about it was really important to Mommy and to be honest about how her heart felt. So I told her my trouble and that it was very hot for Mommy wearing her wig. I asked her if it would be too embarrassing for her if I went to parks for the rest of the trip wearing a ball cap. I will never forget her response. At the early age of six, my baby girl was way beyond her years.

She looked at me and said, "Don't cry, Mommy. You are beautiful without it, and I don't care what people think. I want you to be happy and have fun with me."

I looked at her and asked her how she was so wise at such a young age.

She said, "I am like you, Mommy. We are strong. Please don't be sad anymore."

I put my head down and let my tears flow. All my baby girl wanted was to be on vacation with her mommy and make beautiful memories. At that moment, I realized I was perfect in her eyes no matter what. All of this didn't matter. She wanted me and only me with her whole heart. I told her my sad tears turned into happy tears because of her. I let her know she had saved the rest of the trip. So together we took off the wig, and I put on a hat that she chose. It was a beautiful moment for us both, and we grew without measure from it.

As I was thinking how I was going to leave our room without my security, my sweet McKynna looked up at me and said, "Don't worry, Mommy. I will be with you no matter what."

I gave her a big hug and said, "Let's do this, McKynna."

It was awkward for a while. Honestly, I think others are more uncomfortable with hair loss than the actual person. It was all very hard. I felt somewhat vulnerable, but I got better and better every day. It was hard being at the park's attractions because I felt like the attraction myself and not in a good way. I will say there were a few times that I almost lost it from people staring, but for the most part, it was all good.

I will never forget during one of our visits to the park I was walking next to McKynna and another family member, and there was a person who stood out. For one reason or another, he couldn't stop staring, and he was fixated on me. At the time going without my wig was so very new for me that I had a closed mind concerning why people would stare at me. I took it personally and was extremely defensive. My daughter was the same way. I think she actually fed off of me. She would see me tense up and become introverted. I couldn't believe how she reacted that day. Both she and my family member were vocal and asked the man to stop staring. I started to cry, and it made me sad. I hated myself and the way I looked and didn't know how to deal with all that I was feeling. Not to mention I was trying to set an example for my beautiful, amazing McKynna. I knew no matter how much I tried she would be scared from all this. The question was just how much would it affect her. McGraw was still such a baby I knew it would be less memorable in a lot of ways for him.

 I had to go to the restroom to collect myself and pull it together. I went into a stall, sat down, and cried. Yes, I was feeling very sorry for myself and needed a boost from God at that very moment. I sat there and started to talk to God and ask him to take the hardness away from both me and McKynna. I asked him to reveal the true learning experience from what happened. I knew there was something good to take away from it but just couldn't see what it actually was at that moment. I looked at my beautiful daughter and didn't want this to change her in a bad way. I desperately wanted us all to take something uplifting and inspiring from my illness. I was proud of her for protecting me and for making sure I was comfortable. It was not all right for anyone to make fun of me. If anything, I saw her show all of the strength God gave her.

 Our vacation was nearing its end, and all of a sudden, I noticed my skin had this glowing reddish tint to it. I couldn't really figure out what was causing it but just knew I was red all over my body and it was beginning to itch. Not so bad, and I thought maybe I had gotten a little too much sun.

We packed up and headed home, and I had this sad, sick feeling in my stomach all the way home. I couldn't believe I had to go back and endure all that evilness. It was a hard pill to swallow leaving Orlando and all of its magic and going back to hell. I mean *hell* in every sense of the word. Getting motivated to get on that plane and head back to Indy took every ounce of strength left in me. The only thing I could think about was that I had only two treatments left. I was still thinking that the redness in my skin was an allergic reaction to the sun, especially with all the medications I had in my system.

CHAPTER FORTY FIVE

We arrived home, and as I was unpacking and getting settled, I noticed that the redness had turned into a huge rash. I mean a rash that covered my entire body. I went to Andrew and showed him, and neither one of us had any idea what was wrong. I immediately got nervous and started to worry. I tried to stay calm, but I had no idea what was going on. We were finally moving in to a condo I had found. We had sold the big house., I was so excited that I would actually be taking my last two treatments in a home. I wouldn't have to feel weird any longer, and I could relax.

I had several days before my third treatment, and I wanted to get settled. The rash was driving me crazy, and I couldn't imagine what was going on. Once again my mind started to race, and I tried not to think bad thoughts. The rash just wouldn't let up. I tried over-the-counter medications that did absolutely nothing. I was so tempted to get on the Internet and look it up, but I didn't allow myself to do it. I didn't want my mind to go there again. I went to bed that night and started to think about what it could be. This all felt too familiar, and I began to get so scared. I thought to myself, here we go again. I remembered what my oncologist had told me about the side effects from the chemo. I remembered she had said that you could develop leukemia from it. When I thought about the symptoms of leukemia, I remembered a rash all over your body was a big sign. I didn't know for certain because it had been a long time since she went over all of that with me. I tried to not go there, but after how my life had turned out, I couldn't ignore it. I decided not to say anything of my fears to my mom or Andrew. I wanted to wait and ask the doctor. I had my treatment the next day, and I would wait and not alarm anyone. I was so scared to take my treatment. I really didn't know what was causing it, and it was all over me. I knew that if I could see all the whelps on the outside of my body, the inside probably was one big whelp. I was so scared, and I remember praying every second and asking God to spare me. I tried to divert my thoughts because I had come to know thinking negative didn't help anyone or any situation. I would do anything and everything to make it not true. I had to once again turn it over to him and let him lead the way. I was getting really good at putting my burden and fears on his shoulders. I knew it wasn't good for me to stress or have anxiety at all.

    I got to the cancer center that morning and was in such pain and starting to not be able to breathe. I could tell it was getting very serious, and I had decided I wasn't going to take my next treatment until I found out what was causing it. I had discussed it with Andrew and told him I was scared the chemo might have caused it. He agreed, and I told him I would discuss it with my doctor. The one thing I told myself before I entered that building was that I had to believe in God and in my life. I had to know that it was all going to be all right. THE FIRST STEP TO LIVING IS BELIEVING YOU WILL. You believe it until you aren't here to believe it anymore. Then and only then do you no longer believe. So

I decided I knew it would all work out no matter what. I told myself it was just one more hurdle.

I went in the room, and my oncologist came in. I told her everything that was going on. I explained to her that I was hurting so badly that I could no longer function. I could tell by the look on her face that she was extremely surprised. I knew she had no idea what was going on. She had this very disturbing look on her face. So then I started to panic. She let me know that in all her years she had never seen this and was not at all sure why this was happening. I told her that I wasn't comfortable with going ahead with my treatment until we found out what was wrong. We talked about it, and she wasn't so happy about it because I was already a week behind on my timetable for my treatments. My vacation set me back a little, and you have to get them all in within a certain time frame. I was already pushing it. But I explained to her I wasn't at all comfortable with taking it because we had no idea if in fact the treatment was causing it. I wasn't going to risk it. I can tell you she didn't like that I was questioning her.

I will tell you that I learned so much going through my treatment. All the doctors know is what they have been taught. It sounds very elementary, but it's so very true. They learn what they learn in medical school. It is a practice, and outside of books and classes, all they have are experiences that come their way. They can learn from their patients and what they go through. After medical school it really is all about experiences they go through. I never had to go to the doctor before I became sick. Most people are like me and think they all know everything there is to know about medicine. Through my process I began to realize they are just people too. They do the best they can. I began to understand they don't have all the answers. I believe God gives them the resources to help us but in the end it will be God's will. None of the doctors in my cancer center agreed with my waiting, but I didn't care. All I wanted was to find out what was causing this and why. If it was in fact something in the chemo, why would I keep doing this? Protocol or not, I was the one hurting and suffering. My life was on the line, and again if I didn't do anything about it, no one would. Again, I had to be my own savior.

I let her know it was getting hard for me to breathe and I was scared. She then set me up with an appointment with a dermatologist across the way in hopes we could figure out why this had happened. They got the results, and yes, you guessed it: they had no idea what was causing it. They gave me some medication, and I went home. I was covered in hives, and I hurt beyond belief. I couldn't sleep or eat. I not only had cancer but also this horrible rash all over me that was more painful than you can imagine. I could barely lie on the bed and have my body touch the sheets. My mom did everything she knew to do. Nothing was working, and it really seemed as though it was getting worse. My doctors seemed to become more and more worried as to what was causing the hives. My breathing had gotten so bad that they had to set me up an appointment with a lung specialist. They wanted to run a series of test to look at the inside of my body. At the time I was glad because I couldn't breathe well at all. I had no idea what they were concerned with when they set up the appointment. I really thought it was to give me some medicine to open my lungs. I just wanted something to clear them up.

So I took my mom and the kids to my appointment with me. I was actually so excited because I thought going to a specialist was going to give me some answers. I had gone over to have them take some x-rays of my chest and back the day before. They said it would give them better insight on what was going on. Again I wasn't so alarmed about anything yet. I really thought it was from medicine. But I could tell when we got there that the doctor seemed a little strange as well as the nurse. I wasn't sure why, but I thought maybe it was because I had brought the kids with me. I wanted them with me all the time, and this day was no different. When we got into the room, we sat down and went over a few things, and I will never forget the words that came out of his mouth in front of my kids. McGraw, was still so little that he didn't hear the doctor, but you'd better bet McKynna did.

The doctor looked at me and said, "We need to set up your biopsies."

And I know I looked at him as though he was speaking in some language I didn't understand. I looked at him and said, "I beg your pardon. What did you just say?"

He said, "We need to set you up to have your biopsies taken."

I said, "For what?"

He said, "For the high possibility of lung cancer."

I stood there in complete and utter disbelief. I let him know right away I didn't have lung cancer. I told him I had a chest x-ray three weeks prior and you just don't get lung cancer in three weeks.

He said, "Well, given that you had breast cancer, it is highly possible this is lung cancer."

My entire body was burning, and I couldn't believe what he was saying and that he was saying it in front of my children. I looked at him with tears rolling down my cheeks and raised my voice to him. "I do not have lung cancer. I have hives from an allergic reaction."

He then made me and my mom go look at my test and see my x-rays. I looked at them and to be honest didn't really know what I was looking at. He showed me this huge mass on my lungs, but it didn't look at all like lung cancer or like a tumor. It was a large mass that really had no definition. I went back in the room and let him know I was really mad. I had no idea this was what the appointment was about, and it was in front of my children. My daughter had a million questions and was very worried. I went out to the nurses' desk and made an appointment for the next morning. I was beside myself. I was crying and in a panic. Andrew was in Ohio working, and I had to call him and tell him to come home right away and let him know what was going on.

Before I knew it, I was in the hospital the next morning getting nine biopsies done. I couldn't believe my fate. Are you kidding me? Lung cancer? I was scared to death and so exhausted, and now I would be waiting again to see if the cancer had spread. I laid on that bed before I went in and told my mom that I couldn't take any more. I told her I just didn't understand.

Time went slow, and finally the results came. It was not lung cancer. They did test after test, and I didn't have one precancerous cell in my lungs. It was hives, I didn't know from what but it wasn't cancer.

I got on my knees and cried like a little baby. I had never been so tired and so excited all at the same time. I screamed so loud and thanked God. It was because of him that I was going to make it. I knew at that point that it was time to rebuild Christi. I was in—and all in, at that. When I got the news, it was my second, third, or fourth chance, and I was taking God up on it. I owed him, and I owed him big. I wouldn't let him down, and I would rebuild my temple inch by inch.

The hives were still so bad, and nothing seemed to help. I couldn't live a normal life. I couldn't focus on anything, and when I got hot, it would flare up and become unbearable. I was at the end of my rope and decided to go talk to the lady at my favorite health-food store. I had gone there a lot since I moved there and thought it couldn't hurt. I had tried prescription medication and home remedies. Nothing was working, so I thought maybe the lady that owned it would know what to do.

So I went in and told her my story. I told her how long I had been dealing with my hives. It was like she had seen this a million times. She left us and told us she would be back in a few moments. I stood there with my mom, said a prayer, and asked God to please let her have an answer. I was a complete war zone. I just couldn't handle any more.

So here she came with two items in her hands. In one hand she had a spray, and in the other she had a vitamin. I looked at her and started to cry. I told her I had tried everything and that I was so exhausted from it all. I let her know I would try anything. She said for me to take the spray and use it all throughout the day. I could use it as much as I needed. She let me know it would relieve the itching and discomfort. Then she told me about the vitamin in her other hand and let me know it would get rid of them once and for all.

I looked at her and said, "Can I give you a hug?" I told her I needed a minute to cry. I had just said a prayer that she would have something to help me. Here she was with two things that she said would finally give me relief.

She told me how to take the vitamins and that they would probably be gone in a few days.

I looked at her and said, "I will do exactly what you say, and I am going to believe in it." I gave her one last hug and thanked her from the bottom of my heart.

I got in the car, held my mom, and cried. I was so happy and felt so blessed I couldn't contain myself. My mom was so emotional because as a mom you hurt when your baby hurts. She had been feeling every bit of my pain, and there was nothing she could do about it. I can't even imagine how helpless she must have felt.

We were both so happy we sat there and celebrated, and then I said, "I need to get something to drink. I need to take the cure God just dropped in my lap."

I started taking them, and within three days they were completely gone.

So as I continued to become stronger and get better, I would start to plan my last big surgery, my hysterectomy. My last huge preventative surgery. It was my last big hurdle, and I was ready for it.

I had turned it over to God and had built the relationship with him that I always wanted. I desperately wanted to take the positive from it. The number-one positive thing was I grew so much spiritually, more than I ever thought possible. I know I wasn't the only one the Lord was trying to reach. I know in my heart I was chosen by God as a vessel to inspire others.

CHAPTER FORTY SIX

So I was about to be reunited with my favorite doctor of them all: Dr. Smith. Without him I would not be here writing my story. I trusted him more than anyone I had met throughout my entire journey. Once again, I know in my heart people are brought to us and become a part of our story. We never know how big or little a part they will play, and Dr. Smith played the lead role in mine. Looking back, I understand he was truly the guardian angel I needed, in everything from the education he gave me about the BRCA gene to sending me to the best team of doctors to ensure my life was spared. They are all a result of God's work here on earth. I knew that God was here, but I had no idea how big a role he played in our lives every second of every day. When I met Dr. Smith, I knew he was my saving grace.

So my hysterectomy would be my last really big preventative surgery. I was so ready to get it done because that meant I was one step closer to the end of this horrible nightmare. We made all the plans and had it all in place. The surgery itself was going to take about nine hours. I was doing it in a new way with robots. It was being introduced, and it was a lot better than the old way.

I prayed about it and thanked God I had gotten this far. I was not nearly as scared as I had been during my previous procedures. I wasn't actually taking cancer out of my body, only preventing it from going to a different place within my body. I still had a nagging feeling deep in my gut. I knew they didn't think it had spread to my ovaries, but Dr. Smith said he was going to get in there and make sure he went through it all with a fine-tooth comb. He said he would make sure he looked at every inch of everything.

So I knew I was in good hands, and I trusted him. I knew deep in my heart that he cared and would do everything in his power to keep me healthy. My surgery was coincidentally set up almost to the day a year after I went to his office that very first time. I never knew that first time I met him he would become the hero. He was so handsome and so strong in many ways. So when I thought of him, I thought he was the superhero of my story. I knew from the moment I met him we had a special bond and he was the real deal.

So the morning of my surgery came, and I was ready. I prayed like I always had before all my procedures. I prayed and thanked God for giving great results and for the answer to be that the cancer was gone. I thanked God for bringing me this far and for allowing me to be strong once more. The strength I had shown was most shocking to me. I never knew the strength I had deep in me. We all have it. We just have to know that we do and pull it from deep inside when we need it. We are born with the strength of the Lord; it is up to us to apply it to our lives when we need to.

I will never forget Dr. Smith coming in the room and talking to me before the surgery. It was very early in the morning, and he had to go over the surgery with me. They had me in my gown and had the little shower cap on my head. It was kind of nice because I looked like everyone else wearing that. It was great that he didn't see my head because it was covered up.

Before I knew it, the surgery was over, and I was waking up in my room. I couldn't believe it. When I woke up, the first thing I thought was that I actually did it. I made it through it all. I was not all that I was when I started. I woke up and right away I realized I was bald and looked like I had almost died. I was so pale and so tired. The nurse came in and said Dr. Smith would be in soon to go over everything with me. I was a little nervous because he was going to let me know if he found anything during the surgery. I got ready and tried to put a little makeup on, and I had brought one of my favorite hats. I remembered back to the first day I met him and how different I looked. I had gotten myself looking better than I looked in my twenties. I worked so hard, and I was so proud. When I looked in the mirror as I was preparing for his visit, I couldn't believe that was me. I couldn't wrap my head around it. I had hit rock bottom, and I had no idea if I could ever be that person again. I got in bed and waited for him to come.

I will never forget when he walked in. Again, I thought he was so handsome and his bedside manner was impeccable. I knew that I owed him my life, and I would never forget it. He walked over, greeted my mom, turned to me, and said, "Well, hello."

I could barely look at him because I hated myself so much. I looked up and said, "Oh, hi."

He came over to my bed, sat down, and asked me how I was feeling. Let me tell you how many tears I have shed throughout this entire journey; I wondered some days if I even had any tears left. I looked at him with tears rolling down my face and said, "I am hanging in there." That was really all I could say. I looked at him. "I hope you have some good news for me."

With his sweet smile and gentle voice, he said that everything was absolutely perfect. He let me know that he went over every inch and everything was perfect. He said he couldn't be more pleased. I put my head down and started to cry. I was so relieved and happy that I didn't have the words. My last big hurdle, and it was done. I felt him place his hand on mine, and he said, "You did it. You have come a long way, and you did it, Christi."

I looked at him and said, "I couldn't have made it without you."

He said, "You look great, and you are going to be just fine."

I said, "Please don't say I look great. I know I look like a war zone, but I am alive." Then I thanked him from the bottom of my heart.

Dr. Smith looked at me and said, "No, I need to thank you."

I said, "I am sorry. Why are you thanking me?"

He said, "I am not sure if you are aware of this or not, but you were in my office one year ago almost to the day. The very thing you were in my office telling me you thought you had a year ago, I just removed. I am beside myself that you were so sure you had cancer in your ovaries when in fact you have the very gene that could have given it to you. You might not have had the cancer yet, but you knew in your soul that it was in your future."

I was still crying, and I told him, "Yes, I am very aware of that."

He looked at me and told me that I had forever changed the way he would care for his patients.

I said, "I am sorry. I am not sure I understand."

He said, "Christi, you came into my office, and I saw a young woman who was beautiful and looked to be the epitome of health. I questioned you and truly didn't listen to what you were feeling. I will from this moment on have an open heart as well as an open mind. I have grown as a person and a physician."

I said to him that if my cancer could help one person, it would all be worth it. I looked at him. "Well, I guess it was worth it." I asked him if I could give him a hug, and he said he would be honored. I leaned in and hugged him with all my might. I was crying for the first time because I felt a sigh of relief that my journey was coming to an end.

Dr. Smith got up and said, "Well, this is it, and if you don't write a book about this, I will."

I laughed and said, "You know, I think I might just do that."

I had a few more cosmetic surgeries and office visits, and then the word came. Dr. Wynn gave me the good news that I was finally cancer-free. It was what I had waited to hear since the moment I was diagnosed. I looked up and gave God a smile. I have to say he never let me down and we were quite the team.

I have been forever changed along with Dr. Smith. I have kept my promise to God and to myself. It has been five years, and I give my story to you in hopes that if you or a loved one are going through a terrible journey, my book might give you that extra something you need to survive. I hope that no matter how hard your journey may be, my story can help ease the road a bit. Turn it over to God, and you will be amazed at the work he will do as well as the work he will allow you to do. I hope this in some way brings you courage and triumph.

To Be Continued….

CPSIA information can be obtained at www.ICGtesting.com
Printed in the USA
LVOW06s2322270815

451883LV00004B/301/P